Mary Ellen's

Enough

Guide to Good Housekeeping

^

ALSO BY MARY ELLEN PINKHAM

Mary Ellen's Best of Helpful Hints

Mary Ellen's Best of Helpful Hints, Vol. 2

Mary Ellen's Best of Kitchen Hints

Mary Ellen's Giant Book of Helpful Hints

ALSO BY MARY ELLEN PINKHAM WITH DALE BURG

Mary Ellen's Complete Home Reference Book

Mary Ellen's Clean House!

How to Stop the One You Love from Drinking

Mary Ellen's Help Yourself Diet Plan

Mary Ellen's

Guide to Good *Enough* Housekeeping

by

MARY ELLEN PINKHAM

with Dale Burg

ST. MARTIN'S GRIFFIN

NEW YORK

www.stmartins.com

Library of Congress Cataloging-in-Publication Data

Pinkham, Mary Ellen.
    Mary Ellen's guide to good enough housekeeping / Mary
Ellen Pinkham, with Dale Burg.
        p.   cm.
    Includes index.
    ISBN 0-312-28567-1
    1. Housekeeping.   2. House cleaning.   I. Title: Guide to
good enough housekeeping.   II. Burg, Dale.   III. Title.

TX158 .P56   2002
648—dc21   2001059436

First Edition: May 2002

10 9 8 7 6 5 4 3 2 1

Contents

Introduction

One day, when a friend and I were talking about housekeeping, it occurred to me there was only one really surefire way to keep your house just as clean as you could wish. That's when I came up with Mary Ellen's Greatest Housekeeping Tip Ever: Live alone.

Of course, this is not always possible or even desirable. But I know from experience how much the people you live with can be part of the problem. I could never persuade my son to work for gold stars by tidying his room and, as wonderful as he is, I can't say he was ever interested in housework. My husband tries; he asks me to make what he calls a "Honey Do" list. Am I grateful? No: I'm crazed. My position is, no one's writing lists for *me*. Since everyone else in the house has eyes, why can't anyone figure out what has to be done, and then do it? Imagine how appreciative I'd be. As someone pointed out, no husband was ever shot while he was doing the dishes.

Of course, in my calmer moments I realize that I know what I know—what to do *and* how to do it—thanks to my mom and her mom. Not everyone has this advantage, younger people in particular. Many moms don't want to be stereotyped as housewives and reject learning the "traditional" skills. But dirt happens. Into everyone's life come dustballs, clogged drains, and spills on the carpet. I get inquiries all the time from people who say they don't know the housekeeping equivalent of how to boil an egg. That's what inspired me to write this book.

Sure, there are other books on housekeeping. They remind me of the story of Goldilocks and the Three Bears. Some give you too little—hints and tidbits without the basics. Some give you too much—making every chore seem overwhelming. I've tried to get things just right in this book. It's a real-life guide for people who aren't especially interested in the process of cleaning but want to keep their homes clean and comfortable without much time or help.

When I was younger, I used to clean for other people. I don't mean that I cleaned other folks' homes, but that I worked hard to clean my own because I worried about what people (mostly my mother) would think if I didn't. I can't say I didn't resent this. I even considered leaving a sign in the medicine cabinet that said, "What are you looking at?" But I cleaned the cabinet just in case anyone (especially my mother) did take a peek. (My mother's standards were hard to meet. She once had one of us kids scrub a tree because our dog had mistaken it for a fire hydrant.)

Eventually, thanks to my background, I became a cleaning expert, though I never became a cleaning fanatic. Over time, I have learned to clean for myself in exactly the same way I exercise for myself. I don't enjoy doing it, but I like having done it. Instead of doing a top-to-bottom housecleaning before a party for the benefit of my guests, I save my energy and do it afterward, for my own pleasure. (A bit of advice: The larger and livelier the crowd, the less they'll notice your housekeeping. Just don't run out of toilet paper.)

In any case, my real talent has never been cleaning but finding ways to clean less—to do the work faster, easier, and smarter. Whenever possible, I clean on the fly—while I'm making a phone call or when a commercial comes on TV— because then I don't have to think about it much. I do a little bit at a time, and I bet I don't spend more than two hours a week on routine cleaning. As for the big jobs, I wait until I'm in the mood, once a month or so, and deal with them then. I'm not the kind of person who can schedule a cleaning day in advance.

As it happens, I'm spending less time on cleaning than ever. Why? Because I own less stuff (more about that later). Because new materials make the jobs easier, and so do good products and tools. Because by now, I know what I'm doing. And because I've adopted the idea of "good enough" house-keeping.

Good enough housekeeping means separating what's important from what's not. For example, an oven that's not shiny or a pot that's sooty on the outside is still usable. The food that's cooked in it isn't any less healthy or tasty. There are a lot of jobs where perfect really doesn't matter, either because it doesn't affect the quality of the results or because you'll be doing the same job again soon enough to catch whatever you missed the first time. You're a lot happier when you can learn to say, "That's good enough," and move on.

Cleaning less may actually be a good thing. A lot of problems are created because someone worked too hard—using a powerful cleaning product that caused pitting instead of the mild liquid detergent that would have been good enough, or scrubbing hard enough to take the finish off a surface, leaving it more susceptible to stains.

Furthermore, *The New England Journal of Medicine* reported news almost as exciting as learning that suntans and sundaes are good for you: It is possible to be *too* clean. Young children who have been exposed to common household germs and infections are less likely to develop asthma and wheezing by the time they turn six. In addition, the medical journal *The Lancet* reported that a bacteria commonly found in dust helps kids build resistance by stimulating an immune response.

So think of this as a combination health *and* cleaning book. I'm going to show you that you can help protect your family against disease *and* keep your house in reasonably good shape by cleaning just a few minutes a day. Sure, you'll have to deal with bigger jobs from time to time—but the minutes you spend each day will help minimize even those.

PART ONE

Where to Start

ONE

Dejunk * Defend * Decide

> **Good enough housekeeping** is cleaning
> to your own standards, not to your
> mother's (or anyone else's).

The book is organized on a room-by-room basis according to
my three-step technique.

Step One: Dejunk

"Tidy" and "neat" help you get to "clean." Even the illusion
of tidiness cuts down on the need to clean. If there's a tumble
of cosmetics on the counter or a length of toilet tissue trailing

along the floor, it doesn't matter if you've scrubbed the grout till it sparkles—the bathroom still doesn't look great.

I should also mention the word "organized," though just seeing this word gives a lot of people the guilts. I've noticed that the people who are really good at being organized already are. The majority are just trying. They're the ones who are attracted to the stores dedicated to helping you get organized, where they buy even more stuff.

Having too much stuff is, of course, the biggest obstacle to getting organized.

If you've got 25 bottles and cans scattered around the bathroom, that's 25 things that can spill. That's 25 things that collect dust and dirt. That's 25 things you have to pick up in order to clean underneath.

Put that stuff away.

Better yet, give it away. Or toss it away. Get rid of anything you don't like, need, or use. Whoever said "a place for everything and everything in its place" wasn't thinking about that electric cheese grater you've never taken out of the box. Or the umbrella stand you keep meaning to repair. Or the faded towels that might be useful if you ever do buy that summer cottage.

Not only are these things taking up space, but also some of them require occasional cleaning. What could be dumber than cleaning stuff you don't even like?

The single most helpful way to make housework easier is to have less to clean. What's more, the less clutter there is on a surface the faster you can clean it up.

So the first part of every chapter includes tips to help you tidy up and pare down. Not every one of them will work for you or your home, but every one that does will reduce your cleaning time.

Anyone with an organizational problem is a junk addict. So dejunking may not work the first time around. (It's like giving up cigarettes.) You might have to give each room a couple of passes. And even when you've done that big, initial job, you're always on maintenance. (It's like watching your weight.)

That's because what you have eventually becomes unfashionable, breaks down, or becomes obsolete, and more clutter keeps coming in, thanks to birthdays, holidays, house gifts, flea marketing, and vacation souveniring.

It's everyone's dream to upscale. With the success of my first book, I had that chance. I indulged myself with the fabulous chandeliers with the zillions of crystals to shine, the fancy upholstery so vulnerable to stains, the gorgeous linens that required ironing. Ultimately, I discovered the more upscale I got, the more I was cleaning, because the cleaning people I hired didn't really know what to do unless I was there working alongside them. For me, the biggest difference between having no money and having some money was that when I had more, I was cleaning more expensive things. So I learned my lesson and scaled back down.

Of course, as I've mentioned, you're not in this alone. Periodic clutter control is an all-family responsibility, but the rest of your household may not see it that way. One solution is to wait until they're all away, then start tossing stuff. Last time my husband went on a fishing trip, I got rid of a hat made out of old Pepsi cans tied together with yarn. Who would want such a thing? (Naturally, he went looking for it one day. I told him I wished he'd have worn that hat on our first date; I'd have had some warning what was in store for me.)

What worked even better was telling my family that for my next birthday, I didn't want anything they'd bought or made—just a promise to work with me on a clean-out-the-clutter day.

Step Two: *Defend*

Quentin Crisp has said, "There is no need to do any housework at all. After the first four years, the dirt doesn't get any worse." While that's funny, it's just not true. Ground-in dirt can ruin everything from the rugs to the furniture. Regular cleaning prolongs the life of the things you own and love, sparing you the nuisance and expense of replacing them.

Little dirt problems turn into big ones. When a light coating of dust becomes a layer of grime, you need more elbow grease to clean it off. Worse, you may need a more powerful cleaning agent that can create its own set of problems.

That's why it's important to "defend." That means cleaning defensively; doing a few—very few—essential chores daily or weekly.

Many take almost no time. In seconds, you can remove a smudge from a wall, wipe a cobweb from a corner, dust a lamp, wipe a windowsill. Unless you're living in a palace, you can probably vacuum your living room in less than 3 minutes.

When you clean defensively, housework never becomes a huge and overwhelming task.

Step Three: *Decide*

Step 3 is all about the nonroutine jobs. You don't need any reminder about these because they stare you in the face: the dirty windows, the rust in the toilet, the stained carpet. They remind me of dieting. (Everything reminds me of dieting.) You know when you need to lose weight—it's not as if someone has to tell you—but only you are going to decide when you're going to do it.

It's the same with these jobs. When you decide to deal with them, I'll tell you how. They're covered in the third section of each chapter, though of course some are not unique to a particular room. Wherever possible I've listed several techniques and/or products. It's up to you to decide which seems easiest and/or most convenient.

I have tried to make all the advice clear and simple enough to help motivate you. The fact is, a lot of these jobs require hardly any work at all—for example, just soaking or spraying, then rinsing. (I've marked these effortless jobs with a ✪.) And I promise you, the results will be good enough.

If you're like me, though, sometimes you're willing to put in some extra time trying to solve a problem even when it seems beyond repair. I've included instructions where that might seem worthwhile.

A few words about tips. I made my reputation with helpful hints—many of which I see other people adopting as their own—and I always love a good idea that lightens your work and adds a bit of fun, like these two old favorites: How do you get catsup out of a bottle? Grab it and wind up like a pitcher so centrifugal force brings it to the top. How do you dry lettuce for a crowd? Put it in a pillowcase and let it spin-dry briefly in your washing machine. Naturally, you'll find plenty of hints like these here.

I also like what I think of as Grandma's housekeeping secrets that call for lemon juice and vinegar as cleaning tools, and I became well known for popularizing surprising uses for cola and other common household products. I've also mentioned such secrets here and there when I know they're effective. But just as often, I've suggested commercial products for household problems when they're the most convenient and effective. The real test is what does the job best.

Years ago, I launched Mary Ellen's Home Care products when I came across a product I thought was so wonderful I was proud to have my name on it. The first items in the line were a pair of stain removers (one for bleachable clothes, one for colored garments) that I truly believe are still the best on the market. In addition to Mary Ellen's Formulas 1 and 2 (for set-in stains on white and colored clothes, respectively, there's Bye-Bye Baby Stains Formula 1 and 2, Grease and Oil Remover, Carpet Stain Remover, and For Those Days Menstrual Stain Remover. The other products in my line are also uniquely effective; otherwise, I'd never manufacture them. I mention them here and there in this book along with other products I think are unique enough to mention by name. If you have trouble locating any such products, or you want to bring a special product to my attention, please drop me a line at Mary Ellen Home Products, PO Box 39221, Minneapolis, MN 55439; call 1-800-328-6294; or visit my Web site, www.maryellenproducts.com.

Finally, I think you'll find this book especially practical because it's the product of two minds—mine and Dale Burg's—that don't always work as one, which is a good thing. Many busy people need assistance when they write a book because there's just so much time in the day, but collaborators aren't always acknowledged. Some people like to give the impression they're doing it all and that they know it all. I'm happy to have Dale's name alongside mine because I like to give credit. I believe everyone's success is in some way due to the efforts of other people.

Dale and I have worked together on books and magazine columns for years, and I think readers have benefited from our different experiences. She lives in a modern city apartment, and I split my time between a traditional suburban house and a rural log cabin. She shops in boutique grocery stores and I in giant supermarkets. Our homes are filled with very different materials, so we have different cleaning problems and needs. The ribbed plastic shelf liner that I raved about in my country kitchen turned out to be an annoying dust catcher in her city cupboards. We share a practical nature and we both like to laugh, but we're both stubborn and willing to fight over an idea. Each of us has very strong opinions. Even stronger is our commitment to giving out the best advice we can find. It's on every page that follows.

TWO

Good Enough Housekeeping Basics

> **Good enough housekeeping** is keeping the floor swept to protect it but not worrying if it's clean enough to eat off.

- If you went into a perfectly new house with only vinegar, Bon Ami or Bar Keepers Friend (nonabrasive scouring powders available at supermarkets), and an all-purpose cleaner and used them the way you were supposed to, your house would stay pretty close to perfect: The scale and grime wouldn't build up and you'd never need the potent cleaning products that sometimes create more damage than good. More things have been ruined because they were cleaned incorrectly than because they weren't cleaned often enough.

- For the best cleaning information regarding any particular fabric, appliance, furniture, flooring, or other product in your home, read the information that comes with the product. If you follow the manufacturer's directions, you increase the likelihood that the things you own will look good forever.

- On the other hand, if you have a spill or a stain that seems permanent, it may be worth trying a drastic remedy on the chance you can salvage it. Manufacturers avoid mentioning strong products in a world where people like to place blame—and bring a lawsuit—if there's any sort of problem. Since we seem to be approaching the day when we have one lawyer per person, soon there will probably be no one foolish enough to give out advice and a decline in the number of manufacturers, since virtually everything—from bleach to peanuts, painkillers to hot coffee, and rope to toys—can be dangerous in the wrong context. I am still going to stick my neck out with some unconventional remedies, but let me say this loud and clear: *Always* read the label cautions. And *always* try any solution in a hidden spot so if you run into a problem, you'll be the only one who sees it.

Taking Care

- Be sure you're using the right product. The wrong one may be useless or even harmful. Example: A lot of people use bleach whenever they see a stain. Bleach is very potent and useful stuff, but it can't remove rust. If the manufacturer specifically advises against the use of a product and you go ahead and use it, your warranty may be void and anything that goes wrong may have to be fixed at your own expense.
- Keep this as your mantra: Test in a hidden place. That's because there are so many finishes and so many types of cleaners—and even well-known, well-established brands change their formulas from time to time—so

it makes sense to do a little trial run before you put any substance on your beloved furniture, carpeting, or other possession.

- "Check for colorfastness" is a common warning of mine to remind you to make sure that whatever you're about to apply to your fabric, rug, or wallpaper will not affect its color. Sometimes labels claim an item is colorfast—which means bleach won't harm it—when it's not. So do the test on a swatch or sample reserved for this purpose or in an inconspicuous area. Wet a white absorbent cloth with the solution and gently rub the surface to be cleaned with the dampened cloth. An immediate color change alerts you to potential problems. Otherwise, wait 10 minutes and check again for color change or bleeding by rubbing the area with a white paper towel or cloth. (If a surface has more than one color, check them all.) Some manufacturers recommend that you wait until their product has dried on the spot to check for color changes.

- If other people are helping clean your house, make sure they're using the proper supplies. Never simply assume that people know what they're doing. I had a housekeeper who used a strong chemical cleaner on brass, and another who tossed cushions into the wash with a red towel that ran. Even at best, they may have different cleaning styles and may not be familiar with the products you like to use. I have had more stuff ruined by "helpers" than I like to think about.

- Keep warranties and care manuals for everything you own. Store the folders in inexpensive plastic wall pocket holders mounted inside a closet or cabinet doors. Or use accordion file holders that stand upright in a bookcase or on a closet shelf. Either way, these folders are a lot more accessible than if they're in a filing cabinet, especially if they're at the back of the drawer.

- This being the real world, you may have misplaced the

manual or pamphlet that came with your appliance, furniture, flooring, etc. If you have a computer, you can usually find the company's Web site fairly easily. Often you can just type: www.[fill in name of company].com. There you'll find information and possibly even a copy of the manual you can download. Very likely, you may be able to E-mail the company directly with a specific question. If you don't have a computer, your local librarian or a long-distance operator should be able to help you find the company's address or an 800 number. If you can't get this information, or you don't know the manufacturer, the generic advice in this book should be useful for most cleaning situations.

Basic Rules

- Store cleaning supplies where you need them. To remove a stain or spill, you'll have the greatest chance of success if you deal with it right away, and you're most likely to do this if the tools and equipment are handy. So put your cans and bottles of cleaning supplies in each bathroom, leave a brush in the shower to give the floor a quick scrub when it's needed, and so on. I've listed the tools you'll need on a routine basis for each room.
- Although I'm all for paring down, I'm even more interested in saving time. That's why when it makes sense, I buy duplicates. I have one Phillips-head screwdriver in the toolbox and another in the kitchen, where I use it to tighten the screws on my pot handles or my drawer pulls. I don't want to spend time getting it out of the toolbox or remembering to put it back. I keep one cordless vacuum mounted where it's convenient to both the kitchen and foyer, and I keep another near

the bathrooms and bedrooms. Vacuum cleaners on each floor save a lot of time too. Though the initial outlay is a little more, you'll be giving each piece of equipment only half the normal amount of wear, so over the long haul, your replacement costs will be the same.

Cord Control

Use a 50-foot extension cord on the vacuum cleaner and you'll save yourself a lot of steps. (Buying an extension cord holder for the vacuum is a practical investment.)

Vacuum into a room instead of going out of it and you won't run over the cord.

Blown Away

When you're opening up a vacation house that's been closed for a long period of time, go through the rooms with a leaf blower before you even try to dust and vacuum. You'll loosen up all the dirt.

- Don't overclean. If you polish furniture too much or put too much wax on the floor, you may get a wax buildup that makes the wood look dull.
- Never mix bleach with other cleaning products. You may create toxic fumes.

4 Most Common Household Problems

- *Candle wax melted on something:* Scrape off whatever you can, then point a hair dryer at the spot and blot up the wax, or lay a brown paper bag with no printing on the spot and iron over it.
- *Musty smell:* It's usually mildew, and I recommend several specific solutions in this book. But if the odor persists and you don't know

where it's coming from, call in a pro. Mildew can rot wood, create or irritate allergies, and even be toxic.
- *Crayon on walls:* Crayola recommends WD-40.
- *Label stuck on anything:* WD-40, Goo Gone, or salad oil.

- Invest in the coated disks that attach under furniture and make it a zillion times easier to move and therefore clean underneath. (Some are peel-and-stick; others—for furniture that gets moved a lot, such as chairs—should be nailed in place.) Also, those coated disks save a lot of wear on your floor.

    Ignoring dirt in hidden places is sometimes okay but sometimes not. For example, when little bugs are left to breed in dark, romantic, unlit corners, their babies grow up to attack your clothes. When grime accumulates on the air conditioner filter or refrigerator coils, the machine won't function as well. I'll tell you what else to watch out for.

When to Throw in the Towel

Some common problems with no remedies:
- *Permanent hair dye in a rug:* A rug is made of fibers, which makes it similar to hair or (if it's wool) the actual thing—and the word "permanent" means just that.
- *Yellowed fiberglass:* This happens over time.
- *Dark stains in porcelain tub or on shower floor:* Finish is gone.
- *Yellow stains on kitchen flooring:* If these keep reappearing, they may be due to glue used during installation or discoloration caused by a mat placed on top of vinyl.
- *Recurring carpet stain:* The stain has penetrated to the padding because it wasn't blotted sufficiently. Take up the carpet and replace padding.

(*continued*)

- *Etching on glassware:* Result of hard water or too much detergent.
- *Blue/gold stains on metal drip pans and pots:* Chemical change due to overheating.

- Some stain problems cannot be solved (see When to Throw in the Towel, above), but you can be creative.

  Can you fix it? If a bleach spill has permanently removed color from a rug, do as the pros do and look for a fabric paint or permanent marker that's a close match, and color it in. Wood furniture that is stained can be touched up with crayon, shoe polish, or wax; if necessary, it can also be refinished by you or a professional.

  Can you cover it up? Perhaps you can put a throw rug on a discolored patch of floor or rug, a chenille throw over the spot on a couch that can't be removed, a wallpaper border or wooden chair rail along a wall that's been scratched. Or tile when your heart is breaking: If a hot pot has left an ugly brown stain on your laminate, you can glue a ceramic tile in the spot as a permanent hot pad. (It's probably a spot where you're likely to set a hot pot again.)

- Plan ahead. When you buy furnishings, order enough to put aside "attic stock"—extra yardage of a fabric or rug or wallpaper that can be used as a patch. In fact, if you actually have an attic, you could even staple a piece of the wallpaper to an attic wall so it ages naturally, like the wallpaper hung elsewhere. If you're painting, buy a little extra paint or at least make a record of the number so you can do a touch-up. A squirt bottle (the kind pancake syrup comes in) is terrific for storing and applying touch-up paint. Empty detergent jugs are also great because you can pour a small amount of paint right into the screw-on cap and work with that.

- Make a decorating file with the names and numbers of all your paints, fabrics, etc. Samples and swatches are not only useful to carry along when you're doing additional or replacement shopping in the future but also can be used to test how various cleaning products affect them.
- It's a fact of life that everything needs some kind of maintenance, no matter how "maintenance-free" it's supposed to be. No-wax floors may eventually need waxing. Stainless steel may be stained. Don't wait until the item is on housekeeping life support to call for help. For example if you wait to have upholstery and rugs cleaned until they have more spots than a Jackson Pollock painting, don't expect them to look as if they just left the showroom even if the best pros in the world work on them.
- When your house is such a mess you want to throw up your hands in despair, take off your glasses. Things definitely won't look as bad.

THREE

12 General Tips for Cutting the Clutter

> **Good enough housekeeping** is not
> buying anything until you figure out how
> much trouble owning it will be.

1. Maybe you've finally learned to pick up after yourself. In any case, it will help if you give yourself someplace to put it. The best thing you can do to keep organized is to have a designated place for everything—and I mean *everything*, even the empty shopping bags you accumulate and the mysterious "parts" that probably belong to equipment that's long since discarded. (Try using a pants hanger with clips to hold several shopping bags, and designate a small box as a lost-and-found for odd pieces.)

2. Put up hooks wherever you can. There's no guarantee, but it's possible that less stuff will land on the floor if a hook is handy. (It's probably too late to tell you about this, but it helps to marry a man who's been in the armed forces. He's been trained to hang up his clothes. He's also

been accustomed to standing in lines and may come in handy for this purpose also.)

3. Sort things by category and divide them into separate containers: all the telephone cords; all the electrical supplies; all the things for gluing, taping, and tying; office supplies; sewing supplies; gift-wrapping materials; and so on.

4. Cookie tins, shoe boxes, empty tubs begged from the local ice cream parlor are all suitable for storage, but I really like storage boxes from the local office supply center. They have precut handles and tops that are easy to put on and take off, they're inexpensive (a buck a box), and they're big enough to hold quite a bit but not so big that they're too heavy to lift when full. Also, they're uniformly sized, which makes them look very orderly in your closet, if you care about that kind of thing. It's important to label the fronts so you know what's inside. Use stick-on labels so that when you change the contents (which you'll probably do), you can slap a new label in place. One caution: Use only plastic containers if you're keeping them in a damp place.

5. Here's a no-brainer that may not have occurred to you. Set up your closets so that the things you use most often are easiest to get at. Put the things you need least at the top of the closet and behind other things.

6. Consider how anything will be used when you decide where to keep it. For example, if you use the turkey roaster only at Thanksgiving, free up the kitchen cabinet space by storing the roaster away with your holiday stuff. In fact, I keep the Christmas card list, cards, and holiday stamps inside my roaster, too, because when I'm ready to get it out, it is time to send out the holiday greetings.

7. Be inventive about finding new places for storage.
   • If your home is built with studs and drywall, you can tuck cabinets between the studs.
   • A shallow bookcase just deep enough to hold paperbacks may be built into even a fairly narrow hallway.

Enough

- Pull a sofa away from the wall and surround it with bookcases built to the height of its arms and back.
- Make a sofa for the family room that's built of wooden storage boxes topped with slipcovered mattresses and lots of bolsters. Bonus: You've got sleeping accommodations for guests.
- If the steps to your basement are open, install tracks and a pullout drawer on the underside of one or more. Or replace nailed-down steps with hinged ones and stow items underneath.
- Catalogs and stores do have some genuinely useful storage aids, such as the slim space saver that fits between washer and dryer to hold laundry equipment.

8. Make every closet as functional as possible.
   - Paint the closet walls white. That makes it much easier for you to see what's what and what's where.
   - Put a mirror on the closet ceiling. You'll know what's on the top shelves without having to climb on a step stool.
   - Every home supply store carries battery-operated lights, some incandescent and some fluorescent. If you don't have an overhead light—or if it's insufficient—these are a lifesaver. Another way to bring extra light to a hallway closet without having to run electricity through the closet wall: Hang a track lighting system on the hall ceiling and direct one or more spots into the closet.

9. Don't buy anything without considering whether you *really* are willing to care for it. It's a little like the process of adopting a pet. The puppy may be lovable, but it will have to be walked. Similarly, before you bring home that fabulous chandelier, think about how long it will take to clean those crystals. Ditto for the beige leather sofa, the antique silver tea service, waxed wood, the end tables, and anything that has a lot of parts. I'm not saying to rule

out these choices completely, but think about what you're getting into.

10. Get everything possible off the floor or counter. Mount the toilet or hamper on the wall (search and you can find such things), a restaurant supply house soap dispenser behind the sink, appliances under cabinets, wastebaskets inside cabinet doors, phones and lamps on walls.

11. Box trick: the best-ever solution for hopeless pack rats. When you're doing your clean-out-the-closets thing, pack anything doubtful in boxes, then tape them shut immediately. Neither you nor anyone in the family may look through a box once it's filled or you'll be playing the "I can use this" game. Instead, date the box(es) and put it (them) out of sight. Just make a notation on the box to remind you what category of items are enclosed and to what charity they should be donated. Once a full year has passed and you have not had the need to unseal any of the boxes to search for a particular item, do not open them. Take them immediately to wherever your donation will be welcome.

12. Finally, establish a useful house rule. If something new comes in, something old has to go. This will force you to decide whether you really do need that new whatever and to get real about why you're keeping the old one. Even if you wind up bending the rules once in a while, you have some kind of plan.

Still in the Picture

If you can never find the right time to say good-bye to an item that has outgrown its usefulness—Grandpa's worn recliner, a kitchen table around which memories were made, and so on—take its photograph and place it in the family album. Knowing the picture will be there makes it easier to give the item away.

FOUR

7 Ways to Be More Efficient

> **Good enough housekeeping** is
> managing how to get something clean
> without getting a lot of other stuff dirty.

1. A routing system is key. Find a place to set up a trash container and four boxes: Give Away/Sell, To Go (for return to library, dry cleaner, etc.), Fix, and Mystery Items. When you clean, take a plastic laundry basket along with you from room to room. Along your way, pick up anything that is in the wrong room and drop it off in the right one. At the end of your cleaning, immediately place the remaining contents into the appropriate containers. Encourage your family to make deposits as well, and encourage them to check the mystery box for lost parts, odd socks, etc. Such items can eventually be moved into the trash.

2. Whenever you have to change one lightbulb in an overhead or hard-to-reach fixture, change them all. They were all installed at the same time, so chances are they're

about to burn out at the same time anyway. And while the fixture is down, stick it in the top rack of the dishwasher to clean it (glass fixtures only—not cloth or plastic or electrical parts). Then give the area a shot of cobweb eliminating spray (see p. 44).

3. Use doormats. They cut the amount of dirt tracked into the house by 80 percent, but other than the obvious— preventing footprints on the rug—maybe you didn't know why that was so important. Mats also prevent sand being carried in on shoes. Sand is sheer disaster for many floors, especially tiles and most stone, because it is made of quartz, the third or fourth hardest mineral after diamonds (though not nearly as attractive in a ring). When it grinds into the floor, it scratches and dulls it. Tracked onto a carpet, it wears away at the fibers. People always approach a door toward the side opposite the hinges, so place your doormat off center near the handle. Or get a really big mat. Either way, people will be forced to step on it when they approach the door. Put a second mat inside, while you're at it. It takes about eight steps to get all the sand and dirt off shoes! Make sure you choose an effective mat, with long, thin fibers. These come in a variety of colors. Some mats are too shallow to trap dirt. Also consider removing your shoes at the door and requesting that visitors do the same. You can provide washable slippers in a variety of sizes, if you wish.

4. Plan ahead. Stow extra plastic bags at the bottom of every wastepaper basket so they're already there when you need a fresh one.

5. Maximize your efforts. If you've got the vacuum cleaner out in order to clean the floor, use it to do another little task at the same time: clean out a drawer, chase cobwebs from a corner, vacuum between cushions.

6. Stop problems before they occur. Rinse dishes immediately if they contain food that will dry hard (such as eggs or oatmeal) and you won't be washing them right away.

Discard the junk the minute it comes into the house so it won't litter up your desk. Line the oven with foil when you're baking a drippy pie. Place a vinyl mat under your pet's bowls. Put a bowl under anything that might leak in the fridge.

7. Don't create a mess while you're cleaning a mess. Place newspaper underfoot when you're cleaning the windowsill. Spray the cleaning product onto the cloth or paper towel, then wipe the mirror or the dishwasher so you use less and don't get liquid everywhere. (It's not only a mess, it may damage a gilded frame or the picture inside, or the liquid may affect the controls on an appliance.)

FIVE

17 Tricks to Make Housework Easier

> **Good enough housekeeping** is not washing the dishes before you put them in the dishwasher.

1. Keep the lights dim. It isn't an operating room, it's your home. What people don't see (such as dust in crannies) won't bother them.
2. To keep the wall behind a doorknob clean with a minimum of effort, put a square of clear Plexiglas behind it. Have the hardware store or home center cut it to size, then mount it. No more scrubbing!
3. Have silver, brass, and copper trays, lamps, and other decorative items lacquered so you won't have to polish them. The lacquering will last for up to ten years. (Check in the Yellow Pages under Metal Finisher or Antique Dealer.)
4. Flat surfaces get the most wear. Where practical, have glass tops made to protect flat surfaces such as bedside

tables, sideboards, and other furniture that is vulnerable to spilling. Put felt pads underneath the glass to further cushion the surface. Spots can be quickly removed with window cleaner sprayed onto a cloth, then rubbed onto the surface.

5. Get yourself a washing machine with the biggest capacity your budget can cover. You'll save yourself time by doing fewer loads. You'll also save money, because you won't have to send out large items such as comforters for professional cleaning, and you'll run the machine less often. (There are a few machines that don't even have an agitator, which makes them great for comforters.)

6. Stone surfaces don't require much maintenance. Keep staining problems to a minimum by having the surface sealed if the manufacturer recommends it. A sealer repels water and oil, reduces the absorbency of stone, and minimizes the bonding of mineral deposits in hard water areas. There are many types of sealers on the market; most need to be applied more than once.

7. The greatest invention in the history of housekeeping is the cordless phone, especially a cordless with a headset attachment. While you're passing the time pleasantly chatting with a friend, there's almost nothing you can't do, from cleaning the drawers to washing a window.

8. Tackle a little bit at a time. When you wipe one cobweb, you don't have to go on to remove every other cobweb in the house. Instead of cleaning the entire closet, deal with one shelf. Instead of doing all the dishes in the china cabinet at once, put a stack at a time in the dishwasher along with a regular load. (Or don't do them at all until you're planning a dinner party.)

9. Not for everyone, but a favorite motivator for some: counting the minutes. If you hate repetitive chores, time them to see how long each one takes. Knowing that it will take only six minutes to empty the dishwasher may

make it easier to get started. This sometimes helps with kids.

10. ✪ Tap the power of your dishwasher. It can clean lots of things (if you let them air-dry), including

scrub brushes	combs and hairbrushes
candleholders	kitchen exhaust fan grille
vases	plastic drawer dividers
soap dishes	stove knobs and burner pans
baseball caps	kitchen magnets
plastic toys	rubber and plastic dish drainers
knickknacks	rattan plate holders
hubcaps	heating vents
canisters	some lighting fixtures (top rack only)

Keep small items together in mesh bags, onion bags, or a clean length of discarded panty hose, and turn the water and/or drying temperature down, if possible and if necessary. Use your judgment—you probably won't want to wash the hubcaps and heating vents along with the hairbrushes, for example—and remember that since the manufacturers do not advise cleaning anything but dishes in a dishwasher, you're doing this at your own risk.

11. Clean from the top down, so that the dust will land on the floor. And vacuum last.

Yesterday's News

Before emptying the vacuum bag on newspaper, sprinkle water on the paper so the dust won't scatter.

12. A hamper or laundry cart on wheels, a tea cart, or even a kiddy wagon can travel with you from room to room holding your bucket of supplies. At the same time you

can pick up all the stuff that's in the wrong place and tow it to the right one.

13. There's no point "cleaning" a floor by slopping dirty water around on it. The most effective way to sponge-mop is to carry a spray bottle of cleaning solution along with a bucket of clean water. Do one section at a time, as follows: Spray the cleaning solution down first, then mop, and finally rinse the mop in the clean water.

14. This is very, very important: The secret to getting the best results from most cleaners is to let them stay on the dirty area for 5–10 minutes, or even longer, so they can do their work. (Don't just spray, then wipe them off.) Do another job while you're waiting.

Metal of Honor

Since I found out that you should never wash or polish bronze (chemicals in the water may corrode it, and polish removes the patina), it's become my favorite metal.

15. To make any sweeping job easy, put a plastic bag over the dustpan, then sweep the stuff onto it. Invert the bag, and the mess is neatly packaged to be disposed of. You can use the same method to collect water spills.

16. Three ways to save time with the dishes: (1) Do not wash dishes before they go in the dishwasher. (The manufacturers say it isn't necessary, and it's a waste of water.) But the people who like to do this—my mother, for example—are hard to stop. (2) Do put a colander in the sink and scrape dishes into it: Liquids go down the drain, not into the garbage pail, and large scraps go into the colander, not the dishwasher. Stick the colander into the machine. (3) Do not towel-dry dishes. Not only is it more work, it's also unsanitary. Saving just 5 minutes daily

gives you a whole extra day of free time per year. To dry the dishes in a hurry, you can keep a fan on the kitchen counter.

17. Work your way around the room in one direction—clockwise is usually the most intuitive if you're right-handed, counterclockwise if you're not—and you'll save a bunch of steps.

SIX

5 Ideas for Getting Help at Home

> **Good enough housekeeping** is getting other people to help even if they don't do it as well as you would.

It's very nice that manufacturers have come to the rescue with things like Hamburger Helper, but what we really need is Housework Helper. Or Hamper Helper. Though more women hold paying jobs than ever, they still have primary responsibility for housekeeping—as though having estrogen gives you special abilities to scrub and vacuum. But consider this fact: Though mostly women do the cooking at home, 80 percent of world-renowned chefs are men. Maybe the guys are hiding similar talents for wiping and dusting. Here's how to get some help at home. Put on a sexy nightie. If that doesn't work, you'll need one of the backup plans below.

1. Leave a basket at the top and the bottom of the stairs to deposit items that should be brought up or down—everything from the laundry to the library books. Make it

a house rule to check the basket before going up or downstairs empty-handed.

2. People are often more willing to work when they know the job is close-ended. If you routinely call "work details" that last no more than 30 minutes, you'll probably have an easier time getting everyone to cooperate.

3. If family members aren't diligent about letting you know what grocery items need restocking, ask them to deposit the empty bottle or can, even the cardboard core, in a special "More, please" container.

4. One of my favorite tricks to keep track of paper supplies: Buy a color or pattern you normally never use and put it at the back of the closet. When it shows up, you'll know you're almost at empty.

5. Offer a reward. My generation worked for gold stars, but the ante has gone up. Every time one of the kids does a chore, keep a record of it in a notebook, with a Post-it slipped into a basket, etc. Award "Frequent Helper" points—like frequent flier miles—that pay off in treats.

SEVEN

The Least Equipment You Need

> **Good enough housekeeping** is knowing that just because a little bit of cleaning product is good doesn't mean a lot is better.

If you really want to learn to clean the easy way, the first job you should tackle is your cleaning closet itself. A lot of stuff in there is probably useless, some because it's been sitting around so long that the chemicals are no longer effective and some because it's a brand you don't like or a product you have no need for. Toss any bottles and cans you haven't used in the last six months. (Can't decide what to keep? Move everything into another, temporary spot—even a carton in a closet. As you need and use it, return each bottle to its usual storage area. Whatever's still in that carton after 4 or 5 months, you can discard.)

Following is a list of equipment and solutions that will take care of basic cleaning throughout the house. While I believe in keeping things simple, I recommend you poke around the home center or housewares stores in the cleaning section;

sometimes you find just the thing you need to make a baffling or hard job easier. Occasionally in the book I recommend specific products that I myself have found for a specific purpose. But those I've listed should cover most situations.

Tools

Artgum Eraser/Kneadable Dough. Find erasers at the stationers, dough at wallpaper, paint, and hardware stores. Work dough with your fingers until it is soft and pliable, then use gently, folding it inside itself so that you're constantly exposing a clean side to whatever you're cleaning. It's effective at stain removal but gentle on every surface.

Broom. I prefer to vacuum rather than sweep whenever possible, but you may need a big push broom for the driveway and deck. The long-handled dustpan/broom combo that snaps together is a great idea. They're not usually top-quality, but they're inexpensive enough to replace occasionally, and they're much easier on your back than the short-handled pans.

Broom Tricks
- It's easier to pick up dirt when you spray the bristles of the broom with some water (or furniture polish).
- Put a coat of spray wax on your dustpan, and dust and dirt will slide off easier.
- If your broom doesn't have a rubber grip, cut the finger off an old rubber glove and slide it over the handle. The broom won't fall down if you have to lean it against the wall for a moment.

Brushes. A *toothbrush* won't solve all your cleaning problems, though it's helpful to have one around to use in tight spaces. Keep a *grout brush* handy in the bathroom. The one I like is an automotive wheel brush, square with long bristles and a short handle that makes it easy to manipulate. A big, flat wooden-handled *scrub brush* is for cleaning the tiles themselves. And of course you need a *toilet brush*, preferably self-contained in a holder to prevent drips. Clean out the holder occasionally with an antibacterial cleaner.

Bucket. Instead of a cleaning caddy (which I can't keep organized) or an apron with pockets filled with bottles and tools (who wants to carry around any weight more than what's actually attached to you?), I prefer using a bucket (plastic, because metal is heavy and it rusts). Fill it with your most-used cleaners and tools. If you're in a two-story house, get one for each floor.

Dry Sponge. This tool, made out of specially treated rubber, cleans without liquid. It takes soot off bricks; removes soil from lampshades, walls, blinds, wallpaper, radiators, vents, and acoustical tiles; pulls pet hair off upholstery; picks dust off your computer screen, oil paintings, wallpaper, and TV screens—and more. It takes a light coat of dirt off just about anything, so you can use it to clean surfaces before you wash them. The only thing it doesn't remove is grease. Get two or three at a hardware store, home center, or janitorial supply house; when one's soiled enough to toss in the washing machine, you'll have a spare.

Dusting Cloths. Forget the torn T-shirts and other ways of making do. You need no-lint wiping cloths. Buy 100% cotton towels (the size of a large napkin) at the home store; no-longer-perfect napkins from a local linen service supplier or party rental place; 100% cotton baby diapers; or cleaning cloths from an automotive supply center. Mist them with water, and they pick up dust like magic. Always wash dusting cloths immediately after use. If they're not clean, they're pointless. There are also very effective *magnetic dust cloths*, made of charged polymer fabric, that attract dust and hold it until laundered. These are especially good for computer monitors, television screens, and other surfaces where static is an issue.

Dusting Tools. For cracks and crevices, you need a *small cordless vacuum* or the brush attachment of your canister vacuum. I used to pooh-pooh *ostrich feather dusters*, but I've come around to thinking they're indispensable. They're better than the dusting brush on your vacuum for delicate items such as frames, lamps, and lightbulbs, and particularly those that are hard to reach, like chandelier pendants. Clean the duster by swishing it in a bucket of soapy water, then roll it in a thick towel to absorb moisture and air-dry. *Lambswool dusters* on an extension tool are perfect for dusting in high places, corners, and big areas such as walls and blinds. Some can be machine washed. If yours cannot, wash it by hand. Roll it in a heavy towel to absorb the moisture afterward, and then air-dry.

Dusting 101: The Basics

- Have your feather duster, lambswool duster, and some clean cloths in your cleaning bucket.
- Go through the room clockwise or counterclockwise, depending on whether you're right- or left-handed. Start with a corner and work from the top down.
- Fold the dusting cloth in quarters and use one clean surface at a time. Then fold the dirty portions inside and expose four clean ones. (That's how I'd do it if I were a little more organized. . . .)

(continued)

- Use the lambswool duster for hard surfaces that can take a little pressure, such as baseboards, walls, blinds, etc. Don't move it randomly. Take deliberate strokes downward. Don't forget the baseboards.
- Use the feather duster for lightweight items. Also take deliberate strokes downward. From time to time, hit your leg gently with the duster to dislodge the dust onto the floor (where you'll pick it up in regular vacuuming).
- Be sure to wash dustcloths after each use and your feather duster and lambswool duster occasionally.
- To dust with the vacuum cleaner, adjust the suction control. This is one of housekeeping's best-kept secrets. It's usually that little hole in the front of your canister where the hose attaches. When the hole is closed, the machine operates at maximum suction, which is perfect for a floor. Open it for less suction, which is more appropriate for drapes, curtains, and upholstery. Using too high a setting will put extra stress on your vacuum; using too high or too low a setting may mean the vacuum won't do the best possible job.
- After you've dusted, vacuum the room to pick up all the debris that's fallen to the ground.

Mops. You need two kinds of mops—one for dusting and one for damp mopping. The Swiffer tool comes with dry wipes (for dusting) and wet wipes (for damp mopping). These are handy and convenient, though it's more economical to use a mop with a head that can be laundered, like a Sh-Mop or 3M mop. Both have flat terry cloth heads that can easily be slipped on the handle.

Pressure Washer. This is the single most useful piece of equipment I've ever owned. It's done more for me than my favorite makeup, and if I had to choose, I'd pick it over my dishwasher. If you're a homeowner, it's a must-have. It cleans roof, deck, walkways, pavements, stones, screens, and outdoor furniture. I've even used it in the shower stall. The first one I bought cost a couple of thousand dollars, but these days, you can find a lightweight electric model for $150 that's as good as you'll need. One that provides pressure of 1,400 or 1,500 PSI (pounds per square inch) is sufficient; anything higher may cause damage by removing paint and gouging wood. If only there were a piece of indoor equipment as helpful!

Rubber Gloves. If you're going to use really hot water and/ or strong cleaners, you need rubber gloves. If you don't use them, your nails will look really, really clean, but they won't last very long, and your hands will be dry and chapped. Cleaning solutions and hot water are very rough on hands and nails.

This Idea A-Peels
If the rubber gloves won't come off easily, run cold water over them.

Scraping Tools. To scrape a stubborn spot off any surface without scratching it, recycle an expired plastic credit card. It's relatively sturdy but unlikely to damage any surface. A putty knife is handy as well. For heavy-duty scraping—for example, to get dried paint off a window—you will need a safety razor, a single-edged razor blade in a safety holder. These come in various sizes, and I find them indispensable. Note: Do not point scraping tools straight down when you use them, since they may damage the surface underneath. Instead, wedge the tool under whatever you're scraping off and try to lift it. Always use a lubricating medium (such as oil or water) when you are using this tool to prevent scratches. And make sure the razor is sharp!

Enough
∧

Disposal Method

To get rid of a used razor blade without a mishap, put it in an aspirin tin or a matchbox.

Get a Handle on This

If your broom and/or mop hasn't got a hole for hanging, drive an electrical staple partway into the top and you'll be able to slip it onto a nail. Or screw a cup hook into the broom's tip. Or ensure that the broom will lie flat against the wall if it does have a hole by slipping a large shower curtain ring through the hole, then slipping the ring over the hook or nail.

Sponges/Plastic and **Steel Wool Scouring Pads/Dishcloths.** I prefer dishcloths to sponges for most cleaning tasks, but when you need a little scrubbing power, use a *nylon scrubber* for nonstick pans or a *plastic scrubber* backed by a sponge. Most manufacturers use the same color code for the latter: white plastic for very gentle power, blue for all-purpose, green (heavy duty), and black (heaviest duty, for grills). Use the white whenever possible and reserve the green and black for situations where you don't have to be concerned about scratching. I use soap-filled *steel wool pads* cautiously because they can scratch many surfaces, but where safe, these can save you lots of elbow grease in removing stubborn patches of dirt. Rust-free pads aren't as effective, but the others become unsightly (for remedies, see No-Rust Musts, below). Find the junior-sized steel wool pads that you can use once and toss, or cut the larger pads yourself. Bonus: When you cut them, you'll sharpen your scissors at the same time.

No-Rust Musts

To rustproof the steel wool pad:
• Store the pad in a small clay flowerpot.

- Or keep it in a plastic bag in the freezer. (Slide the pad only halfway out, and you have a plastic "holder" to protect hands.)
- Or rub both sides of the pad on a bar of Ivory soap, then place it on a holder that allows air to circulate and dry it out. Dampen it before use. A soapy pad is less likely to rust, and as a plus, you're less likely to get metal splinters.

Scour Power

- If you've got a scrubbing job and there's no scouring pad on hand, crumple aluminum foil into a ball.
- Or use an onion bag.
- Or put a sponge in an old stocking to get more cleaning power.

Squeegee. This tool makes cleaning windows and shower walls much, much, much easier. But buy the right kind. On cheaper versions, the rubber usually extends beyond the blade, which causes a lot of streaking. Look for a thin, narrow blade with the rubber flush against it. Recommended: Ettore Pro-Series Master Squeegee. Or buy a professional-quality squeegee from a janitorial supply house. Best size: 12 inches, unless you have small windowpanes. Don't buy a squeegee with a foam scrubber at the other end. The foam drips.

> "I'm not going to vacuum until Sears makes one you can ride on."
> —Roseanne Barr

Vacuum Cleaners. You may need two vacuums. A *canister* is a bit of a pain because it's clunky to drag around, but the canister attachments are essential for cleaning sofa cushions, drapes, windowsills, under the fridge, and inside drawers. To handle a lot of carpeting, you need an *upright* with a beater bar, which deep cleans. Actually, I vacuum my kitchen and bathroom floors with my upright Oreck vacuum even though they advise not using a machine with a beater bar on bare

Enough
∧

wood floors. I've been doing it for thirty years without a problem and you may want to do the same. (As I've said, manufacturers are very cautious when they give out advice, but I think sometimes you have to be guided by common sense and experience.) My Oreck is lightweight and small enough to fit into tight spaces. It's expensive but worth the splurge. Or look for a reasonably priced rebuilt model. Or check with a local janitorial supply house and see what they recommend that fits into your budget. Another possibility is an electric broom. These aren't for heavy-duty cleaning, but they may be sufficient for a small apartment with little or no carpeting. They're lightweight, and the dust cups (which are used instead of bags) are easy to empty after each use. Buy only the kind that can stand alone, not one you must lean against a wall.

Bag of Tricks

When a vacuum salesman comes to your home to demo a vacuum, he often throws down some dust and uses both your old vacuum and the model he's demonstrating to compare how well they work. Naturally, the new one works better—but one reason it does is that the salesman always uses a new or nearly empty bag. That's the key to effective vacuum cleaning. Some say never to use a bag that's more than one-quarter full, but I'm more forgiving. Use it up to half full.

• If you haven't got a fresh vacuum bag, here's an emergency solution: Just cut off the bottom of the old one and empty it. Then fold and staple the bag closed.

Defective Work

• Do you suspect that your vacuum cleaner isn't pulling up the dirt properly? To check its effectiveness, sprinkle talcum powder on a dark carpet and try to vacuum it up. You'll be able to see how well it's working.

• Is there something clogging the vacuum hose? Use a straightened wire coat hanger to poke it out. And *never* vacuum up those pack-

aging peanuts you spilled all over the floor when you excavated a tiny gift from a big box. They are exactly the right size to clog a hose.
• To protect your walls and furniture, put some foam weather stripping around the edge of your vacuum.

Wet-Dry Vacuum. If you have a carpet, you need a wet-dry vacuum that can suction up liquids because the first thing you should do about a spill is blot it up. Many of the stain-removal problems associated with spills are caused when the initial spill isn't blotted thoroughly or is rubbed into a larger area. The old wet-dry vacs were industrial machines, but now you can get small cordless ones. While they can pick up a fair amount and there's no fear of shock since they're cordless, they must be cleaned after every wet use, which can be a bit messy. I personally love the Bissell Little Green Machine, to which I was introduced when I did the infomercial. It doesn't just suck up spills—it also applies the stain-removing solution and the rinse liquid. This can be a carpet lifesaver.

Window-Washing Tools. You'll need Ettore squeegees and an Ettore window scrubber plus a three-compartment caddy. (See Windows, p. 189.)

Cleaners

Economy Moves
Look for concentrated cleaners at your local home center. I recently bought a 64-ounce container of glass cleaner for $7. Since each ounce can
(continued)

be mixed with water to make a quart of cleaner—and quarts cost around $3 in the supermarket—the savings are tremendous. (And if you're like me, you'll blow the savings on beauty creams that aren't worth it either!)

Abrasive Cleaners. Baking soda is a gentle and natural abrasive, and if you buy (or put it into) a shaker container, it's very convenient to use. Bon Ami is similarly gentle, and for stain removal, much more effective on many surfaces, including fiberglass, imitation marble, and plastic. It's recommended by many manufacturers, including Corning, Farberware, Pyrex, Regal, Rival, American Standard, Americast, Sterling Plumbing Group, and West Bend. Bar Keepers Friend is another fabulous, non-scratching abrasive. It's particularly useful to remove rust.

All-Purpose Cleaners. For most general cleaning, I recommend a light cleaner such as Shaklee's Basic H or whatever neutral pH cleaner the local janitorial supply house is selling, preferably in a spray bottle for easy application. Ordinary liquid dishwashing detergent mixed with water is a fine cleaner, too—about 1 tablespoon to 2 quarts of water—but if not sufficiently diluted, it may be too sudsy to apply through a spray bottle, and it's not recommended for a floor (because it can leave a residue). A little goes a very long way. You'll also need a heavy-duty degreasing cleaner such as Simple Green from time to time.

CAUTION: When the product label says wear gloves and/or a mask, do it. I don't freak out easily, but one day as I rubbed on hormone cream to relieve my hot flashes, it dawned on me that since I had faith the cream could penetrate my skin to do its work, why didn't I believe the bad stuff could do the same? Now I'm in full getup when using strong chemicals.

Ammonia. Get plain ammonia, not the kind with suds. (Ammonia with suds often leaves streaks.) Add a couple of capfuls to a quart spray bottle filled with water as a glass cleaner. Also, before you use brand-name oven cleaner, loosen the grease in your oven by filling a glass bowl with ammonia. Leave it in the cool oven overnight in a well-ventilated room, then wipe off the grease in the morning. The extra step is worth the trouble. You may not even have to use a heavy-duty oven cleaner afterward.

Automatic Dishwasher Detergent and **Detergent Rinse Agent.** I like the powder rather than the gel. Shake the box to make sure it's not lumpy when you buy it—if it's lumpy, it's not as effective. If you have very hard water, use a liquid rinse agent as directed, and use the dry rinse agent also. We have very hard water in our cabin in northern Minnesota, and even though we have a water softener, I had spotty glassware until I used the liquid/dry combination.

Bleach. You probably have this on hand for your laundry needs, but bleach is also the most effective mildew remover. I had heard that there was little difference among brands, but I found that was not true when I developed a bleach-based product called Mary Ellen's Stain Remover Formula 1 to remove tough, set-in stains from white and colorfast items. My favorite brand is Clorox. CAUTION: Never use bleach on aluminum, metal, or silverware, which it may cause to discolor. Bleach also can eventually cause grout to deteriorate. Bleach is powerful stuff and should be used with care, always diluted with water.

Carpet Spot Remover. Naturally, I recommend my own Mary Ellen's Carpet Stain Remover. Of the other widely available products, I like Spot Shot and De-Solv-It (which was good enough to be used on the Alaskan oil spill). Read the labels, because you will probably need two types of products, one that's best on protein stains such as food and drink and one for the greasy stains such as latex paint, oil, and crayon.

Cobweb Eliminating Spray. These are products that spiders hate. When spiders stay away, so do cobwebs. Make sure you purchase a brand that is safe for indoor use. Find these in home centers, department stores, and catalogs.

Put a Sock on It

Cut off the elastic part of a pair of old socks. Pull them over your shirt-sleeves and push the sleeves up if you're going to get them dirty or wet.

De-liming or **De-scaling Cleaners.** You need these in the bathroom for soap scum and mineral buildup if generic products (vinegar, baking soda) don't work. Lime-A-Way or Santeen, Chrom-R-Tile, and Scrub Free (for soap and scum) are useful. I use Clean Shower preventively. You just mist the shower walls with it and you don't have to rinse, wipe, scrub, or squeegee. (Caution: Not recommended for refinished tubs, natural stone, or natural marble.)

Dishwashing Detergent. For hand-washing dishes and other cleaning. See All-Purpose Cleaners, p. 42.

Disinfecting Cleaner. Reserve this for the places where bacteria are likeliest to be a problem—around the toilet, under the sink, in the toilet brush holder, in the trash compactor. Research indicates that the more freely we use sprays like this, the more the germs build up an immunity to them.

Dry-Cleaning Fluid. This is what you use when the cleaning instructions (as for upholstery or carpets) call for a solvent remover. Energine and Carbona are two that are widely available. Follow the instructions on the bottle.

Glass Cleaner. Buy the concentrate in a home store (see Economy Moves, p. 41). Or use 3 tablespoons of white vinegar to a cup of water. Or use windshield-washing fluid, which is less expensive than commercial glass cleaners.

Glue-Removing Solvent. These products, such as De-Solv-It and Goo Gone, are petroleum based and remove tape residue, tree sap, wax, adhesive residue, and bumper stickers. Though salad oil and lighter fluid can be used in lieu of a commercial product on certain surfaces, the latter is flammable and neither is appropriate for carpeting or upholstery.

Laundry Detergent. You can use this to remove stains from carpets and upholstery. See Upholstery, p. 185.

Murphy Oil Soap. This cleaning standby has been around long enough to collect Social Security but is still a great choice for cleaning wood (especially kitchen cabinets) and stripping through layers of grime and old wax. It's also good for cleaning leather and vinyl and more. It's gentle yet tough on dirt.

Oven Cleaner. Easy-Off is my favorite. Follow the instructions on the can. Most important: Leave it on as long as possible, since the longer it works, the better job it will do. Wipe away any remaining film with vinegar on a cloth. If the fumes bother you, use the no-fume formula or try the treatment described under Ammonia, p. 43.

Upholstery Shampoo. When you need a water-based upholstery cleaner, you can use laundry detergent or buy upholstery shampoo that comes (basically, suds only) in a can. See Upholstery, p. 185.

Vinegar. This is a weak acid that can etch marble and other stones. But it is inexpensive and "natural" and a very effective all-around cleaner. I mix 1 quart of water with ¼ cup of vinegar in a spray bottle and keep it handy for kitchen counters, the bathroom sink, and other lightly soiled surfaces.

Good to the Last Drop

Need to get the last bit of cleaning fluid out of a bottle with one of those spray pumps? Put some marbles in the bottle to raise the level of the liquid.

Stuff You May Need

Cream of Tartar. This natural product is used in making candies and cookies, so find it, in powdered form, with the spices in the grocery store. It's a mild acid that is sometimes used in home remedies for cleaning and polishing metals.

Fels-Naphtha Soap. This bar soap for heavy-duty cleaning is having a comeback. Normally a homely little grocery item that sells for $1 or so, it's also in fancy boutiques for several times that. Sometimes you can find it with the bath soaps (because the clerks don't know any better), but it's usually with the detergents.

Furniture Cleaner, Polish, Wax, or **Oil.** If your wood furniture has a polyurethane finish, you can just wipe away smudges with a damp cloth. But follow your manufacturer's recommendations. See Furniture, pp. 177–182.

Furniture Scratch and **Nick Cover-up.** I like Old English Scratch Cover, which comes in two colors, one for light wood and one for dark. Every once in a while, I use this on my baseboards and sometimes on my beat-up coffee table. It covers the faded areas, too.

Hydrogen Peroxide. An environmentally healthy alternative to bleach, it's usually sold in dilute form. In the drugstore, you will find 3% hydrogen peroxide, which is what is used in all the home cleaning remedies. (To clean hot tubs, you may require a 35% concentration, which is very strong and corrosive. It can be bought where swimming pool supplies are sold.)

Laundry Prewash Spray. Removes food stains on hard surfaces as well as fabrics. (Use it on siding if Halloween pranksters have egged your house. But take photos for insurance purposes, since protein can cause staining.)

Mineral Spirits. A paint thinner sometimes used as a dirt and grease remover. Very toxic and flammable. Use only in a well-ventilated area, and wear rubber gloves (which you should throw away or wash thoroughly with hot, sudsy water afterward). Leave a cloth with mineral spirits to air-dry thoroughly before discarding. Don't wash it in the machine or put in the dryer because it could catch fire.

Scouring Stick. Works when the strongest chemical products fail, and it's safer than any of them. A scouring stick is pumice stone, a natural abrasive. Use it to remove rock-hard mineral deposits; stubborn rings in the toilet bowl; scale and rust on metalwork and piping; lime and algae deposits in swimming pools; unwanted paint on tile, masonry, and concrete; baked-on food, grease, and carbon buildup in ovens, barbecues, grills, and iron cookware. Find it in hardware stores and home centers.

Silver Cloth/Silver Polish. Personally, I don't keep silver for the same reason I wouldn't have a long-haired pet. They're pretty but too high-maintenance. But if you like silver, you need a cloth and/or paste. Although Seeds' Merit Silver Polish is what Tiffany's reportedly uses, I prefer the more widely

Enough
∧

available Hagerty Silver Foam. After you use this one-step tarnish remover and polish, the item should be washed with soap and water and dried. (Once the paste cleaner has dried out, though, replace it, because the concentration of abrasives is too high.) A silver polishing cloth (like Birks or Hagerty Silversmiths' Gloves) can be used and reused on lightly tarnished, decorative silver (like a candlestick), but if you use it on items meant to handle food, wash them afterward with soap and water. Now there's also an easy-to-use product named Connoisseurs Silver Wipes that come in boxes of ten disposable dry cloths, each of which cleans about three five-piece place settings.

Dips are quick and nonabrasive, but they may cause pitting. In any case, never leave items in dip longer than recommended—usually only about 10 seconds—and never use dip on pieces that have wood or ivory attachments. Some people feel that the dips make the pieces so clean that the silver looks like stainless, but that wouldn't bother me. My only complaint is that the bottles don't come large enough to let you dip a whole serving tray.

Homemade Silver Polishing Cloths

Cut a cloth diaper or 100% cotton restaurant napkins into squares. Dip them in a mixture of 2 parts ammonia, 1 part silver polish, and 10 parts cold water, then hang them to dry.

Give It the Brush

Slip a rubber band around the silver polish bottle or jar and slip a toothbrush through it so it will always be handy to tackle the little crevices.

Steel Wool. Grade 0000 steel wool is for buffing, polishing, and paint removal on furniture and other delicate surfaces, and it can be used to clean glass, chrome, and porcelain. This item comes from the hardware store and is not to be confused with soap-filled steel wool pads used in a kitchen.

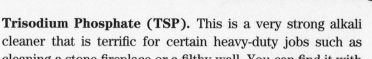

Trisodium Phosphate (TSP). This is a very strong alkali cleaner that is terrific for certain heavy-duty jobs such as cleaning a stone fireplace or a filthy wall. You can find it with the paints in the hardware store. Follow the cautions on the bottle. Mex is a phosphate-free alternative to TSP.

Washing Soda. A heavy-duty, somewhat toxic cleaner (read the cautions on the box) found in the laundry section of the supermarket. It's primarily a detergent booster and an odor remover. It also cuts grease, removes stains, disinfects, softens water, and may open drains.

Wax and **No-Wax Floor Products.** You don't need these for polyurethane floors or new no-wax or ceramic tile floors. They don't make the floors nicer, they just make them more slippery. They also create a buildup that's a real pain to remove. You may need them if you have wax finish floors or old no-wax floors.

WD-40. A multipurpose product that lubricates, protects metal from rust and corrosion, penetrates stuck parts, and displaces moisture. It also removes grease, grime, and marks from many surfaces.

Tools to Know About

Friends and fans are always telling me about new tools they love, such as a carpet rake to pull up pile, an "up and over" vacuum attachment for cleaning high-up shelves, and a plug-in device that provides warm air to damp closets. Write me at Box 39221, Minneapolis, MN 55439 or visit my Web site, www.maryellenproducts.com and I'll help you locate these and any other housekeeping item I've mentioned or you're curious about. Also write me about your own favorite tools and cleaning products. I'm always on the lookout for anything new and great.

Enough
∧

Stuff You Probably Don't Need

Drain Cleaner. Prevention is the best approach. Use strainers or bits of net or pieces of steel wool in every drain, and pour boiling water down the drain once a week. Never pour chemicals down your drain. In the best case, you're dealing with a toxic substance; and in the worst case, the clog won't dissolve and you've got a mess to clean and a plumber bill to face. See Drain Solution, p. 120, for preventive measures, and Drain, Clogged, p. 134, for remedies.

Dusting Spray. If you dampen your rag or mop, it will hold the dust as well as a commercial product made for this purpose. (Remove any streaks with a dry cloth.)

Liquid Abrasives and **Foaming Cleaners.** They just make a mess. See Abrasive Cleaners, p. 42.

Toilet Bowl and **In-Tank Cleaners, Tablets.** Unless you're cleaning a nursing home or a nursery school toilet, those cleaners are much more powerful than you need. The tablets make the bathroom smell like bleach, and do you really find that fluorescent blue toilet water enhances your decor? You can manage without these. In fact, American Standard, for one, warns against in-tank cleaners and says that bleach products in the tank may cause damage.

And definitely any product you haven't used in a year. It's probably lost its effectiveness anyway. I give you permission to get rid of this product along with the unworn microminidresses hanging in your closet. (The micros may make a comeback, but your thighs probably will not.)

PART TWO

The Good Enough Ways to Clean Every Room in Your House

EIGHT

The Bathroom

> **Good enough housekeeping** is agreeing that the hygiene requirements for a bathroom aren't the same as for an operating room.

I was relaxing in one of my favorite spots—my whirlpool bath—and it occurred to me how odd it is that the smallest room in the house often seems to require the most amount of attention. In fact, the bathroom should be the easiest of all rooms to clean, because so many of the tasks can be done in 30 seconds or less, "as you go." Example: While the kids are bathing, you can keep an eye on them and manage to clean the sinks, mirrors, and counters at the same time. And as always, the less clutter, the faster the cleanup.

Dejunk

PROBLEM: Shampoo bottles, medications, and cosmetics all over the counter, windowsill, and bathtub rim.

- First, get rid of the medicines, prescription and otherwise, for ailments that bothered you years ago. Products past their expiration dates may be useless or even dangerous. Most have expiration dates on the prescription label, on the label, or on the crimp of the tube. If in doubt, trash the stuff. Please note that there are also expiration dates on items such as hydrogen peroxide, iodine, and even sunscreen products.

- Then give or throw away the beauty products you won't be using. If you've bought new products, chances are it's because the old ones didn't live up to their promises. Fortunately, some can be recycled: Unwanted shampoo can be poured into the liquid soap container and used for washing hands or for hand laundry. And combine all leftover conditioner into one bottle and smooth the mixture onto your legs before you give them a shave.

- All that old makeup can go too: the blue eye shadow, the false lashes, the Cherries in the Snow lipstick, and the other blasts from the past. They're not meant to last forever—fashions change.

- No matter how much you've trashed, there will someday be more. So get the largest medicine cabinet that will fit in your bathroom. The more stuff you can put behind closed doors, the neater the bathroom looks and the easier it is to clean. Plus, a big mirror makes the bathroom look bigger.

- Make a cosmetics organizer for the medicine cabinet with a piece of 2-inch-high wood that's the appropriate length and width to fit a shelf. Drill holes the right size to hold lipstick brushes, etc. Cover the sides with paint or paper, the bottom with felt pads or contact paper.
- Instead of or in addition to a larger medicine cabinet, hang a see-through shoe bag behind the door and use it to stow toothpaste, hair spray, shaving cream, etc. Or use a spice rack, placed at adult eye level.
- Easier than hanging a shelf: Put up a nail and hang a shower organizer to hold anything you want to get off the counter.

Beauty Spots

Putting your powders and liquids in glass containers may not reduce the actual clutter in your bathroom, but it will reduce the visual clutter—and that helps too. Look for old laboratory flasks with their ground glass stoppers at yard sales or lab supply shops.

PROBLEM: Extra soap, toilet brush and holder, cleaning products, etc., stuck in the nooks and crannies of the room.
- Add storage space: a vanity under the sink or a small cupboard, the bigger the better. It can also store extra soap, sanitary supplies, that giant bottle of mouthwash, and so on. If the vanity hasn't got a shelf, add one.
- Stow the tub toys in the vanity. Cut a piece of foam rubber to fit the floor of the vanity and just put the toys in there. Don't bother to wait for them to dry. The foam will absorb any moisture.
- Hooks inserted into the underside of the vanity top and the inside of the vanity walls and doors can hold your curling iron, blow dryer, and drawstring bags containing curlers, ribbons, clips, etc.

PROBLEM: No place to stow extra toilet paper.

- Remove one end of two three-pound coffee cans, then stack them and use duct tape to seal seams and hold the cans together. Cover to match bath decor and presto, you've got a toilet paper storage unit. Use a plastic lid on the top (which you can decorate with ribbons, flowers, etc.) and one on the bottom too (to prevent any rust marks).

- Refrigerator soda holders also hold four rolls of toilet tissue. Fasten them under the shelf in your linen closet. (You may have to bend the top wires to attach them to the shelf properly.)

PROBLEM: Towels all over the place.

- In the past, when I was young and foolish, I was a major purchaser of bath towels. I couldn't pass up a white sale. Then I developed Pinkham's Law of Bath Towels, which states that the number of bath towels your family uses in a week is the total available supply. So instead I bought my husband, my son, and myself white terry cloth robes with names embroidered on the pockets plus a couple labeled Guest #1 and Guest #2. Result: one robe per person in the weekly wash instead of a zillion towels. Get the kind with hoods, so no one needs a separate towel for hair drying.

- It also helps to assign each person a different color towel. When there's no confusion about which is whose, perhaps they won't reach for a fresh one.

- Store small towels rolled up in a wine rack or basket, or go into an office supply store and buy yourself some of those wall-mounted file holders that are tilted at a 45-degree angle and use them to stack towels. Or buy small, hotel-type wall-mounted towel racks that can hold hand towels and washcloths.

- Great space saver: a double-sided hook that slips over

the shower rod. One side can hold the bathrobe, the other a towel, a washcloth, or a second robe.

• I use a fresh washcloth twice a day and I hate having them hang all over the place, so I have a plastic container in the vanity where I toss used ones, and I launder a batch twice a week.

PROBLEM: Towels hanging sloppily from the rod.

• Sew the ends of a towel together, slip it over the towel rod, put the rod back in the brackets, and you have a rolling towel. Great in homes with little kids.

• Replace bottom screws of towel racks with cup hooks. Hang small towels and washcloths from them.

• Or get the towels out of the bathroom. Mount towel bars behind doors in family members' bedrooms so towels and washcloths can be kept there.

PROBLEM: Clutter caused by items drip-drying on the shower rod.

• Install a second shower rod directly over the tub, behind the present shower rod. Use it for drip-drying clothes right out of the machine, to hang garments that have come in from the rain and snow, and for air-drying rubber bath mats and damp towels. Everything's hidden behind the shower curtain.

PROBLEM: Hair dryer occupying too much space on the bathroom counter.

• Find a holder that fits the "beak" of the dryer. A round washcloth holder or a holder meant for the toothpaste cup might be the right size.

• Or install a wall-mounted dryer. This is a safety as well as a clutter issue: A hair dryer that can be knocked into the toilet or tub is a safety hazard.

Enough
^

If It Gives You the Slip

To stop the shower caddy from sliding over the showerhead, cut a piece of old garden hose about 1½ inches long and slide it over the pipe in front of the caddy. If the hose doesn't grasp the pipe snugly, put a few drops of epoxy glue inside and glue it in place. Or put a fat rubber band around the neck of the showerhead in front of the caddy to prevent slippage.

PROBLEM: Constant gunk on the soap dish.

- Use liquid soap on the counter and body wash when you bathe or shower—no soap dish needed.
- Or make your own soap on a rope—it takes only a few minutes and can be used over and over. Sew a pocket for the soap from a bit of toweling or washcloth and attach a rope so you can hang it from a hook in the shower stall or on the wall above the tub. (Catalogs that sell bath accessories also sell such a product.)

PROBLEM: Toilet paper unfurled across the bathroom.

- Squeeze the roll to flatten it before putting it on the holder. It won't unroll as easily when Junior or Fido plays with it.
- Or put the empty cardboard roll inside the new one before you slip it over the holder. It won't spin as easily.

Stack 'Em Up

If you fold the matching washcloths inside the hand towels, your closet will look organized and you'll have both when you need them.

PROBLEM: Wastebasket looks messy.

- Install a small, kitchen-type basket inside the door of the vanity.
- Leave extra bag liners at the bottom of the basket so a spare is handy when you toss a full one.

Stuck on Itself

When the shower curtain seems glued to another portion of the same curtain, toss it into a dryer set on low or air-dry for a few minutes.

Handy Wipes

Hang a roll of paper towels in the bathroom. You'll quickly find many uses for them—to wipe a counter clean, absorb a spill, buff a shine, defog a mirror. Mount the holder inside the door or tuck it away inside the vanity (hung vertically if it doesn't fit horizontally).

PROBLEM: Peeling decals on tub bottom.

- Spray them with oven cleaner, wait 15 minutes, scrape away as much as possible (with a plastic credit card or other gentle tool or with a safety razor, if you keep the surface wet), and remove the residue with WD-40.

PROBLEM: Toiletries and toys lined up all around the tub.

- Get a basket made of rubber-coated wire that's meant to hook under a shelf, then bend the hooks in the opposite direction so it will hang over the side of the tub. It can hold shampoo, tub toys, and more, and water won't puddle or soap build up beneath it.
- If you have counter space alongside the tub, gather up assorted items in plastic containers. Drill a hole in the bottom so they can drain.

PROBLEM: Magazines scattered on the bathroom floor.

- It's everyone's secret: The john doubles as a reading room. At least someone's reading in your house! Magazines and books can be slipped onto a towel rack screwed into the wall 6–8 inches from the floor, under the toilet paper dispenser. Better than a basket: no need to clean it.

If You're Thinking of Buying or Remodeling

DO'S in a Bathroom:

- A lift-off showerhead that can be handheld—what Europeans call a telephone shower. This item is great to help you clean the tub and walls, even rinse off a trayful of china or glass knickknacks, or wash down a high chair or screen, since you can direct the spray where needed. (Useful on bodies for the same reason.)

- Grout that's colored and as thin as possible. I imagine that colored grout gets as dirty as white grout, but who can tell? As for the narrower grout lines, they mean less hard-to-clean grout area.

- The biggest tiles possible (because that also reduces the amount of grouting). Ignore the conventional wisdom that you can't use large tiles in smallish spaces; they may look amazingly good. (Try having them installed in diamond shape, rather than parallel to the walls; the room looks much bigger.)

- A "banjo" top that goes around the sink and extends over the toilet seat. The good news: more counter area. The bad news: may attract clutter.

- Paint with a matte finish (or wallpaper). It shows dirt much less than a wall done with glossy paint. Oil-based paint is a must for bathrooms and also kitchens, since wiping doesn't wear it away.

- A single faucet backed by a pressure-balance valve. It blends hot and cold water so that you can adjust the mix perfectly. (New York City requires such faucets as a safety measure to prevent burns from scalding hot water.) Even better is a more expensive thermostatic mixing valve. You can set it to maintain a specific temperature and it allows water to flow at a higher rate than an ordinary pressure balance valve.

- As I suggested before, wall-hung hampers, even toilets, are spacesavers and dirt minimizers.

- A laminate floor. It's durable, easy to clean, and water-resistant, and it eliminates any grout-cleaning problems.

DON'TS in a Bathroom:

- Lots of glass in the shower. You'll see every handprint and every water mark—so if you have hard water, you're in for it. Those beautiful, glass-filled bathrooms look great in the model houses, but of course no one actually takes showers in the bathrooms in model houses.
- Sinks with tiny grooves and niches. They catch dirt.
- Sinks that are too shallow. You get lots of splashes on floor and walls.
- Those "new" sinks with bowl only and no counter. They're beautiful but impractical (a combination that has many parallels in other life situations). Where do you put the makeup, comb, etc., while you're grooming yourself? True, large counters encourage clutter, but there is such a thing as too minimal.
- Marble. Another beautiful but impractical idea. It's very fragile, and I hear from lots of people about the problems they have removing scratches and stains.
- Sliding doors in medicine cabinets. A pain to clean when dirt collects in the tracks.
- Textured surfaces. They trap dirt. Same goes for those bathtub appliqués.
- Dark tiles and fixtures. These show every mark. They also scratch easily.
- A gigantic bathtub. It can't be cleaned unless you climb inside.
- Fancy wastebaskets that need liners. Why would you spend a lot of money for a basket and then put a plastic bag in it?
- Big wastebaskets. A lot of trash is more unsightly than a little trash.
- Brass fixtures, gold-plated fixtures—in fact, any fixtures other than chrome. The lacquered ones peel; the others are a pain to clean, and they don't wear well.
- Wall-to-wall carpeting. Yuccck. You know how dirty a tile or vinyl floor gets, so although it might not be obvious, imagine what's growing in those fibers. The carpeting is so bulky the only place to clean it is by hanging it on the wall in a car wash.

THE BASIC SUPPLIES FOR GOOD ENOUGH BATHROOM CLEANING

Abrasive cleanser
All-purpose cleaner
Bleach or other mildew-removing product
Bucket
Cordless vacuum
Cleaning cloths
Disinfecting cleaner
De-liming or de-scaling cleaner
Rubber gloves
Squeegee
Sh-Mop or Swiffer
Toilet brush/holder

DAILY
CLEAN THE SHOWER WALLS AND DOORS.

- After showering, mist the shower stall with Clean Shower. (Not recommended for refinished tubs, natural stone, natural marble.)
- If you can't or don't want to use this product (some people think it leaves a residue), hang a squeegee in the shower and encourage everyone to give a swipe to a couple of walls when they're done. (A squeegee is better than a towel, because it doesn't require laundering.)

WHY: The biggest bathroom cleaning problems—mineral deposits, mildew, and soap scum—all are the result of water remaining on a surface until it evaporates. Wipe away the water and you eliminate the problem. Preventing hard-water deposits from building up is quicker and easier than cleaning them off.

VACUUM THE FLOOR.

- Use a cordless vacuum to pick up hairs daily or as needed. If you don't already have one mounted in or near the bathroom, get one. (A wet-dry model is a help because you don't have to wait until the floor is dry to do your sweep.) Or haul the vacuum in when you're vacuuming elsewhere. CAUTION: If you're vacuuming stone, be extra-careful to move the nozzle just over the surface, not bang into it, because the stone can be scratched.

WHY: Because floors aren't meant to be hairy.

Multitasking with the Vacuum

- Use it to clean hairbrushes.
- Use the hose to clean whiskers out of the electric razor.
- Suction out dust from the vanity drawers and corners.

CLEAN THE TOILET BOWL.

- Use the brush alone, or to remove stubborn stains, clean the bowl with disinfecting cleaner.

WHY: The more frequently a toilet bowl is brushed, the less likely scale and mold will build up and deposit, thus reducing the need for chemicals altogether. Besides, you don't want visitors to talk about your Toilet of Shame.

WIPE THE SINK AND COUNTER.

- Wipe up any spills immediately and wipe the counter dry.

WHY: The biggest bathroom cleaning problems—mineral deposits, mildew, and soap scum—all are the result of water remaining on a surface until it evaporates. Wipe away the water and you eliminate the problem. Preventing hard water deposits from building up is quicker and easier than cleaning them off.

Ring Mastery

- Keep a shaker filled with baking soda at the edge of the tub and shake a little in the bathwater to prevent a ring whenever you bathe.
- Or pour a little generic baby shampoo into your bath. It eliminates ring around the tub, and as a bonus, you have a bubble bath that costs pennies.

WEEKLY

CLEAN THE COUNTER AND SINK.

- Use all-purpose cleaner, wipe with cloth.

WHY: Remove any dirt daily wiping left behind.

WIPE THE VANITY OR UNDERSINK AREA.

- Wipe with a damp cloth and all-purpose cleaner.

WHY: To prevent grime buildup.

CLEAN THE MIRRORS.

- Spray glass cleaner onto a paper towel, wipe the mirror, discard the towel.

WHY: So that you can see yourself. On second thought . . .

MOP THE FLOOR.

- Whether your bathroom has a resilient floor (such as vinyl or rubber) or a hard floor (such as tile or marble), it should be damp-mopped. Use a Sh-Mop or a Swiffer with a wet wipe. If you can't get to the whole thing, just cover the high-traffic areas.

WHY: This prevents surface dirt (that isn't picked up by the vacuum) from being ground into the floor. Grit is very abrasive and can do a lot of damage.

CLEAN THE TOILET AREA.

- Clean this area last, as it is the most likely to be germy.
- Pour disinfecting cleaner in the bowl and let it stand while you clean the rest of the area.
- Use more disinfecting cleaner around base of the toilet, then use a clean cloth to rinse. (Afterward, clean these cloths in the washing machine with hot water, soap, and bleach.)
- Brush toilet clean, flush. Leave the brush in bowl, add a few more drops of disinfectant cleaner, and use the brush to wipe out its holder. Put brush back in toilet, flush to rinse it, and return it to its stand.
- Use disinfecting cleaner on a paper towel to clean under and on top of toilet seat.

WHY: The area around the toilet is where germs are most likely to thrive—especially if you have men in the house. (They leave the seat up, too.)

Hair Net

- In the bath, stick a little bit of netting into the tub drain to catch the hairs. Replace the netting once in a while. A good tool to get it out? A fondue fork. Or look for a brush made for this purpose. It's long, narrow, and flexible.

MY READERS TIP ME OFF: Hard-Water Protection

- People who live in areas where hard water is a problem tell me they find it worthwhile to apply Rain-X after they clean glass shower doors, plastic laminate counters, sinks, floors, windows that are likely to be splashed with hard water from a sprinkler—basically any unpainted nonwooden surface. The application lasts for months and causes water to bead off, preventing mineral deposits and soap scum.

- An alternative treatment is to clean and dry surfaces, then rub shower doors with baby oil, or cover everything from ceramic tile walls to the shower door—except the tub bottom because it will be too slippery—with floor, furniture, or car wax, then buff them. (If you're using wax, use one of the cheaper brands; these usually have more silicone.) This seems like a lot of work, but if your hard-water situation is extreme, it may be worthwhile. Preventing deposits may be easier than cleaning them off.

Decide

I've listed the most common bathroom problems, in alphabetical order, below. Decide which ones are important to you and try the following solutions.

ACRYLIC SHOWER FLOOR OR TUB

- Follow manufacturer's instructions. Cleaning is simple because mold and mildew don't grow on acrylic. Use an all-purpose cleaner or a 50/50 solution of vinegar and water in a spray bottle, spray on, and rinse off with a soft cloth. If the stain is stubborn, try whitewall cleaner or prewash spray, such as Shout, leave for half an hour, then scrub and rinse.

- The real secret to keeping acrylic looking good is to make sure it doesn't get scratched. This means avoiding strong detergents, strong abrasives, and any other product not specifically mentioned by the manufacturer. Don't use ammonia, Tilex, or aerosol cleaners, since the propellant will cause cracks and void the warranty. Many disinfectants and other products will cause damage. Even a liquid detergent container resting on the surface can cause staining.

- Use only cloths or the softest scrubbing pads on these surfaces. Some plastic scrubbers can scratch acrylic.

- *Dull:* Auto rubbing compound can restore shine, but rub gently, taking care not to rub through thin-colored gel coat. Marine wax can give it high gloss. But don't wax shower floors, since that makes them too slippery. Or use Gel-Gloss, a protective coating made for acrylic. Any of these takes extra time to apply but provides protection that's probably worth the effort.

- *Hard-water stains:* See Removing Hard-Water (Mineral) Stains, p. 69. Don't use any product unless the label indicates it is safe for acrylic surfaces.

BATH MAT, RUBBER

- Spray on whitewall tire cleaner, leave it briefly, scrub, then rinse.

- Or machine-wash it, but let it air-dry, preferably in the sun.

- Or use a pressure washer on it.

Enough
^

BATH RUG, FABRIC

- Machine launder with a mild detergent. Machine dry. But air dry a rug with a rubber backing, which may crumble as a result of high heat.

Go to the Mat

- For a quick pickup of hair on the bath rug, slip on a rubber glove, then run your hand across the mat. Hair is drawn toward it like a magnet but won't stick to the glove.
- A dry sponge will also pick up hairs quickly.

BRASS FIXTURES (OR HINGES ON TOILET SEATS), TARNISHED

Brass looks good but needs constant attention—every fingerprint shows. I warn everyone not to buy brass, but if you're checking here, I guess the word didn't get out to you.

- Don't ever use strong abrasives.
- If the fixtures are lacquered, just clean them with a damp cloth.
- If unlacquered, use Brasso or other commercial metal cleaner.
- Or use ammonia to remove stains.
- The home remedy is a paste of equal parts salt, flour, and white vinegar, or lemon juice and salt. Use a cloth to rub it on, rinse, and dry. Ammonia can also remove stains: apply, rinse, dry.

Bugs in the Bathroom

If you have pests like silverfish or water bugs in the bathroom, use an insect-repellent spray and send a shot into the corners of the bathroom where cobwebs may be a problem.

Removing Hard-Water (Mineral) Stains

High concentrations of calcium and magnesium form hard deposits on porcelain enamel, ceramic tile, fiberglass, chrome, and glass; manganese produces brownish and blackish stains; and iron may cause red stains.

- Do not use abrasives on shiny surfaces, because when they're worn down, they're harder than ever to clean.
- Avoid bleach, which will eventually remove the shiny finish on porcelain enamel and may cause grouting to decompose.
- Start with the mildest remedy, such as dishwashing detergent or another neutral pH cleaner.
- If those fail, try the home remedies that use mild acids to remove hard-water deposits:

    The classic home remedy for hard-water stains is vinegar (a mild acid) and water, sprayed on, then wiped off.

    You can remove toilet bowl stains by pouring cola or lemon Kool-Aid in the toilet and leaving it overnight or by sprinkling a layer of Tang around the bowl and flushing or brushing away stains after an hour. There's no magic to these: Cola contains phosphoric acid and the others contain citric acids. A paste of borax and lemon juice is even more effective.

    Blue stains caused by copper in the water or copper leaching out and being deposited at the drain opening can be eliminated if you wet the stain with 3% hydrogen peroxide, then give it a general sprinkle of cream of tartar. After 30 minutes, scrub and rinse.

- Alternatively, use a commercial de-liming or de-scaling product such as Lime-A-Way. For rust stains, try Zud, Super Iron Out, or CLR, then rub with a wet sponge or cloth. Make sure the label of any commercial products says it's safe for use on the surface where you are going to apply it.

CERAMIC TILES

- To remove soap scum and hard water deposits: First run your shower with very hot water for a while before you use any cleaner. The steam will help loosen dirt so it will come off faster. See Removing Hard-Water (Mineral) Stains, p. 69.

- For really stubborn film on the shower stall, rub with dry 0000 fine steel wool (from the hardware store; not the same as the soap-filled steel pad). Rinse afterward.

- Whitish powder may appear at time of installation or periodically at later dates. Known as efflorescence, it's just a layer of water-soluble salts that you can brush off or leave alone, since it eventually disappears. Some people recommend an acid wash, but this may leave an off-white deposit that's even more resistant to being removed.

- Tiny ceramic tiles are often seen in the bathrooms in very old buildings and frequently used on shower floors and left unglazed so they aren't slippery. Because they're porous, they stain easily, but they shouldn't be cleaned with harsh abrasives.

    If the small tiles look very bad, the good enough solution may be to regrout with a thin layer of grouting, then seal.

    For a more thorough job, you need a cleaner with phosphoric acid. Follow the cautions on the label. The most stubborn stains may require a poultice cleaner—a chemical or cleaner mixed with a white absorbent powder to form a paste that's like peanut butter. With a spatula, apply a ¼- to ½-inch layer on the surface, then put a piece of plastic on top and leave it for a day or two. Ask your hardware store to recommend the ingredients for the poultice.

- See Grout, Stained, p. 73 and also Ceramic Tile Countertops, p. 127, for other stain removal suggestions.

CHROME

- *Fingerprints and smudges:* Use all-purpose cleaner or baking soda on a barely damp cloth, sponge, or paper towel; or use spray glass cleaner or liquid dish detergent and water.
- *Soap gunk around chrome fixtures:* Soak a paper towel in white vinegar, squeeze, and wrap it around the chrome for 10 minutes. Wipe dry.
- *Stubborn stains:* Try baking soda or a tartar-control toothpaste and a little elbow grease. Don't use harsh abrasives.
- *Tarnish:* Stick with spray glass cleaner, liquid dish detergent and water, or rubbing alcohol. Don't use harsh abrasives.

CORIAN

See p. 130.

CULTURED MARBLE

- *Dull:* You need a commercial gloss renewer. (A complete new finish cannot be applied, however.)
- *Hard-water deposits:* See Removing Hard-Water (Mineral) Stains, p. 69.
- *Scratches, chips:* You need professional rebuffing with a mixed gel-coat compound.

DRAINS, CLOGGED

See p. 120 and p. 134.

FAUCET HEAD, CLOGGED

• If water is squirting out of the faucet rather than running smoothly, sediments may have accumulated in the little filter screen inside. First cover the end of the faucet with a washcloth (so it won't get scratched), then use pliers to unscrew the end of the tap that contains the filter. Soak the screen, washer, and end of the tap in boiling white vinegar. Wash with liquid dishwashing soap and water, and pick out anything that remains with toothpick or cotton swab or fine piece of wire. Replace the pieces, and your water should be flowing smoothly again.

• If you can't figure out how to remove it, pour some vinegar into a plastic bag and fasten the bag over the faucet head with a rubber band. Leave overnight, then rinse. Flow should be more even—and water may even taste better.

FIBERGLASS

• Follow the manufacturer's instructions. Most stains can be removed using one of the all-purpose cleaners recommended by the manufacturer. Apply it, leave it for an hour, then rinse.

• *Hard water:* See Removing Hard-Water (Mineral) Stains, p. 69. If you use a commercial product, make sure the label says it's safe for fiberglass.

• *Soap scum on:* If all-purpose detergent doesn't remove the stains, use Bon Ami or Bar Keepers Friends on a damp sponge, or rubbing alcohol.

• *Scratched:* Sand the area with fine-grit (1200 grit) wet-dry sandpaper. Buff gently with a soft cloth and toothpaste or baking soda if you don't have rubbing compound or car wax. Rub in a circular motion.

• *Tar, oil paints, or similar:* Get a commercial fiberglass cleaner at the supermarket or from a boat dealer.

A Dimple Plan

If you have a dimpled-bottom fiberglass tub, get fine (120 grit) drywall sandpaper from the home supply store. (It looks like window screen.) Mix 3 parts baking soda to 1 part borax, and apply it with the sandpaper. (Don't use this remedy on smooth surfaces.)

FIXTURE, CEILING

✿ If it needs more than dusting, take it down and put it into the dishwasher. (Most fixtures are dishwasher-safe if you put them on the top rack and turn the machine to air-dry.)

GOLD-PLATED FIXTURE

• Wash with all-purpose cleaner, buff dry with soft cloth. Use ammonia to remove tarnish, but be sure to rinse and dry it afterward.

GROUT, STAINED

• If you see black (and sometimes red) spots, you've probably got mold or mildew, a common bathroom problem.
• First try liquid detergent and water.
• If that fails, use a mildew-removing product.
• If other remedies fail, and you're not allergic or asthmatic, wear a mask and rubber gloves, leave the windows open, and use a solution of 1 part bleach to 10 parts water, with a little liquid dishwashing detergent added to cut grease or dirt. This remedy should be used only infrequently, because excessive treatment with bleach may cause grout to disintegrate, making it even more vulnerable to mildew.
• To go beyond good enough, remove the mildew, then use a combination stain/sealer. The seal will help pre-

Enough
^

vent mildew plus mildew and oil stains, though it won't repel dirt. Resealing every six months will help, and ultimately it's easier than trying to clean this stuff.

- Or repaint. See Grout Expectations, below.
- And prevent future problems. See Mold Story, below.

Mold Story

- Mold and mildew thrive in dampness, create a really unpleasant, musty odor, and can do permanent damage. Prevention is critical.
- Keep surfaces clean. Mildew can start growing even on greasy film.
- Keep surfaces as dry as possible.
- Don't leave wet clothing, towels, etc., hanging around.
- Leave the shower door slightly open even if you have a vent.
- Keep a bathroom window open a crack.
- Use a ceiling fan, a small fan, or an exhaust fan where appropriate. In very humid situations, invest in a dehumidifier.
- Use a heater to keep the room dry in the winter.
- When you spray on mildew-preventing disinfectant, don't wipe it off. Let it dry in place.
- Keep silica gel in drawers and closets.
- If your problem resists do-it-yourself remedies, call in a mold abatement specialist. Some molds are toxic, but even if they aren't, they can create allergy problems and/or cause damage to your home that insurance won't cover.

Grout Expectations

One way to solve the problem of dirty-looking grout is to paint it. I would suggest using a dark color rather than white. Follow these instructions for applying and testing the paint to make sure it will adhere.

- If necessary, buy a product at the tile supply shop that will remove wax or sealants already on the grout. Also purchase the paint of your choice and sulfamic acid.
- After you've used the remover (if necessary), apply the acid, fol-

lowing instructions on the label. Wear gloves and follow the cautions on the bottle, applying the acid to the old grout with a scrub brush. Rinse thoroughly a few times. Let dry.

- The next day, using a toothbrush as an applicator, paint a small section of the grout with the new color. With a hair dryer, dry the paint.
- Press a piece of masking tape onto the area, then pull it away. If color adheres to the tape, your grout won't accept recoloring. But if little to none of the new paint sticks to the tape, continue painting. This recoloring job may keep the grout in great shape for years.

LAMINATE COUNTERTOPS
- For routine cleaning, use a mild all-purpose cleaner. Never use cleaners containing acid, alkali, or chlorine on laminates. Since some countertop cleaners contain these ingredients, as do drain cleaners, bleach, rust removers, and lime scale removers, read labels before applying any product to your laminate. For stain removal, see Laminate Countertops, p. 140.

LIGHT SWITCH
- A circle of handprints around a light switch and the dirty switch itself—these are two of my pet peeves. Use a mild all-purpose cleaner and a damp cloth, and if you need more power, Bon Ami or Bar Keepers Friend. A toothbrush is helpful to work out embedded dirt.

MARBLE COUNTERTOP, SHOWER FLOOR
- See also Cultured Marble, p. 71. Marble should be sealed, since it is easily harmed. Ask your hardware store to recommend a good sealing product. Most brands of sealer require two coats.

- *Dull:* May be residue from soap and all-purpose cleaner. Surface may require a professional cleaning and resealing.
- *Etched spots:* If an acidic cleaner on marble has caused etching, wet the surface with water and sprinkle on marble polishing powder, available from a hardware store or your local stone dealer. Rub the powder in with a damp cloth or use a buffing pad with a low-speed power drill. Continue buffing until the etch mark disappears and the marble surface shines. If the results aren't good enough, call in a pro.

Stains on Marble

If I had marble countertops or floors (and I wouldn't—too much trouble), I'd try a commercial marble stain remover whenever I had a stain, and if that failed I'd just phone a pro. But if you want to go beyond good enough, here are some ideas.

- *Food stains:* Treat like oil stains (below) with the 3% hydrogen peroxide treatment.
- *Mildew:* Get a disinfectant cleaner made especially for stone from the hardware store.
- *Oil stains:* They're usually circular, often dark at the center.

   Wash with ammonia, rinse thoroughly.

   Or mix mild liquid dishwashing detergent, water, and some flour into a paste the consistency of jam. Spread it on the stained area, then cover it with plastic wrap and tape down the sides with masking tape. Leave overnight, remove the plastic, and let the mixture dry, then scrape it away.

   Or make a paste of 3% hydrogen peroxide from the drugstore and powdered whiting from the paint store. Keep it damp by covering it with plastic wrap sealed with masking tape. After 10–15 minutes, rinse with water. Repeat if necessary. Buff.

- *Rust:* An orange or brown stain. Mix commercial liquid rust remover and whiting from the paint store and follow the instructions above for oil. Rub marble with a dry cloth.
- *Soap scum:* Mix ½ cup ammonia with a gallon of water. Frequent or excessive use of solutions containing ammonia solution may eventually dull the surface of the stone. Alternative: a non-acidic soap scum remover.
- *Water spots:* When hard water evaporates it leaves spots with mineral deposits that bind to stone. Soak a few white paper towels with a solution of 3% hydrogen peroxide and leave covered with a piece of plastic for 15 minutes, then rinse. Or from a hardware store, get a neutral pH stone cleaner plus a stone polish if you have polished marble.

DON'TS for Marble

- Take care not to spill soaps and shampoos that contain dyes, oil polishes, soft wax, and/or medicinal shampoos. They may discolor it.
- Don't use a rubber-backed mat on a marble floor. It may cause permanent staining.
- Avoid soap with a high lanolin content. It causes more filming and therefore more hard-water deposits.
- Acidic cleaners such as lemon and vinegar may etch marble, and alkalis (such as Tilex, bleach, baking soda, and ammonia) can make the surface rough.
- Powdered cleansers, mildew and mold removers, and disinfectants may also cause damage.

MEDICINE CABINET SHELVES, RUSTING

- Use a commercial rust-removing product or use a soap-filled steel wool pad.
- Then line with contact paper to make wiping easy in the future.

- Use can "cozies" meant for soft drinks to hold shaving cream, spray, and other cans, or put plastic lids from chip cans on the underside of cans, both in the cabinet and on any other bathroom shelf.

Pickup Sticks

Inexpensive disposable chopsticks or wooden skewers are useful in the bathroom. Use them to break up a clot of tissue in the toilet or to pick something out of the drain.

MY READERS TIP ME OFF: Cleaning High Places
A reader who's 5-feet tall says she had trouble cleaning the tall mirrors in her bath until she got one of the long-handled squeegees—foam covered with net—that they use in gas stations to clean car windshields. Now she sprays on the window cleaner, uses the long-handled tool to scrub with the foam side, and then squeegees off the dirt.

MIRROR

- *Coated with hair spray:* Use rubbing alcohol or paint thinner (diluted) in a well-ventilated room.
- *Streaked:* Use a commercial glass cleaner. The home remedy is to dip a cloth in plain vinegar, rub it on the glass, and wipe it off with newspaper. Or spray a mixture of 1 tablespoon ammonia and 1 quart of water on the mirror, and wipe it with a clean dusting cloth.

ODOR

- The quickest, easiest, least expensive room-deodorizing solution is to light a match.
- There's a plug-in charcoal filter with an on-off switch, just twice the size of a switchplate and costing about

$20, which I highly recommend for the bathroom. It has all those perfumed deodorizer deals beat by a mile.

- If you have to postpone doing the laundry, sprinkle the contents of the hamper with baking soda. But if the hamper odor is strong, you may have mildew growing like a Chia pet. Don't procrastinate any longer.
- A chronic musty odor in the bathroom indicates mold and mildew. Don't ignore it or try to mask it. See Mold Story, p. 74.

MY VIEWERS TIP ME OFF: Stained Bathtubs

I've been told that with a hopelessly dirty tub of any type, a thick layer of laundry detergent smeared on, left for a couple of hours, then rinsed, will solve the problem. A solution of last resort is to spray it with oven cleaner from the bottom up. Let set 15–20 minutes, then rinse. Try this at your own risk.

PLEXIGLAS ACCESSORIES, SMUDGED

- These items scratch very easily, so you need a soft cloth and a special cleaner, not conventional glass cleaners. (Of course the very fact they need a cleaner of their own is a pretty good reason to get rid of this stuff.)

MY READERS TIP ME OFF: Hiding Bathroom Rust

This may not be the most glamorous solution to the problem of a rusty plate where the toilet pipe enters the wall, but it beats anything else for economy. Take a margarine tub and cut it all around, about ½ inch from the bottom. Take the bottom piece, make a hole the same diameter as the pipe, and cut a slit in the piece so you can slip it over the pipe.

Enough
^

PORCELAIN ENAMEL

- Don't use abrasives, which eventually make porcelain more vulnerable to staining. For stubborn stains, apply a mild solution of chlorine bleach for 15 seconds, then rinse. Alternatively, use commercial cleaners.

To Reglaze or Not to Reglaze?

In the past, "reglazing" involved covering the surface of the tub with an epoxy paint that over time would peel, chip, and bubble. New urethane coatings provide a better finish, come in many colors, and are much less expensive than installing a new tub. Reglazers can do walls, floors, and the sink as well as the tub, and some guarantee the job for ten years. If you're considering this, check out the company's references carefully, get the best warranty you can (from a company that's been in business for a while), and make sure they observe the cautions while doing the work (since it's toxic). Fumes may cause you to become ill, so leave windows and doors open to vent and plan to vacate your home for at least four hours after the coating is applied.

SHOWER CURTAINS AND LINER

- Soap scum can be removed from plastic shower curtains by machine washing. Fill the washing machine with warm water, add ½ cup each of detergent and baking soda, then put in the curtain with two bath towels. Run through the entire wash cycle, and add 1 cup of vinegar to the rinse water. (Do not wash out the vinegar.) Take the curtain out before the spin dry cycle and hang it immediately or, if it's very prone to wrinkles, warm it for a few minutes in the dryer, then hang.
- For fabric curtains, observe instructions on the label.
- Mildew on plastic curtains can be removed with a cloth dipped in alcohol or a diluted solution of bleach. If the mildew on the bottom edge of the curtain resists being removed, trim it away with scissors. Repeat if

necessary. If the shower curtain gets too short, just add a second set of curtain rings below the first. Keep the curtains open in order to reduce the risk of mildew.

- Or just buy inexpensive liners and replace them when there's a problem.

The Hole Story

- You can reinforce or mend the holes in shower curtains by taping over them with strong, clear packaging tape, then using a hole punch to make a new hole.
- There are also commercial kits for repair.
- I love the newest shower curtains that have slits on the top. They slip over the shower rods and there's no need for rings.

Attack of the Shower Curtain

If that curtain routinely comes after you in the shower, attach a little bit of Velcro to the hem and a companion piece to the wall of the shower or tub.

SHOWER DOOR

- If all-purpose cleaner doesn't remove mildew or hard-water stains, use a commercial product specially made for this purpose. After cleaning, lemon oil makes the door shine and resistant to future soap buildup.

SHOWER DOOR TRACK, SCUM IN

- Remove the doors by lifting them up, then clean underneath. De-limers or de-scalers will clean the tracks, and the best tool is one of those foam rubber "brushes" sold in the paint department. A handheld shower attachment is great for flushing out debris from the tracks. Put a towel on the floor to catch any overflow.

Enough
∧

SHOWERHEAD, CLOGGED BY HARD-WATER DEPOSITS

- If the showerhead is metal, boil it in a solution of ½ cup vinegar and 1 quart water.
- If the showerhead is plastic, soak it in a solution of ½ cup vinegar and 1 quart hot (but not boiling) water.
- If the showerhead cannot be removed, pour the vinegar and water into a plastic bag, use a rubber band to secure the bag to the showerhead, and leave it in place for a few hours.

MY READERS TIP ME OFF: Ceramic Tile Wipes

A fan from Pittsburgh says she keeps the tiles clean by wiping the walls with a fabric softener sheet after showering, and when she goes into the shower next, she rinses and wipes dry. No soap buildup for weeks, she claims.

SINK

See Acrylic, Fiberglass, Porcelain Enamel, etc.

TILE

See Ceramic Tiles.

Super Bowl

If you're going on an extended vacation and have a problem with hard water, you shouldn't leave standing water in the toilet. So turn the water valve off, then pour a bucket of water into the toilet, which causes it to drain. No deposits will form, and you've saved yourself a lot of work.

TOILET, RIM HOLES CLOGGED

- (This is only for folks who have serious hard-water problems. Everyone else can skip to the next topic.) You'll probably need to check these with a mirror since they're not visible from above. The best tool for cleaning them is a coat hanger or a nail, but if you can't resolve the problem and need a drastic solution, go for heavy-duty San-teen De-Limer and Toilet Bowl Cleaner.

TOILET, STAINED

- See Removing Hard-Water (Mineral) Stains, p. 69. If you are using one of the commercial remedies, first pour a bucket of water into the toilet (which causes it to empty out). Or see if you can empty it out by sticking the toilet brush in and out of the bottom a few times, which works like a plunger; repeat several times until it empties. Turn off water to the toilet, apply the commercial remedy to the stain, leave for a half hour, and brush. If the stain remains, empty out the water, then go over the ring with a scouring stick.
- For very serious stains, you may need heavy-duty San-teen De-Limer and Toilet Bowl Cleaner. Handle with caution.

TOILET SEAT, SPOTS ON

- Use mild, soapy water, then rinse the seat thoroughly with clear water and dry with a soft cloth. Avoid detergents, disinfectants, or cleaning products that come in aerosol cans, and steer clear of chemicals or abrasives that may damage the seat's finish or stain. (For the fewest problems, never buy a wood or padded seat.)

TUB

See Acrylic, Fiberglass, Porcelain Enamel, etc.

TUB TOYS, SOAP SCUM ON

- Run them through the dishwasher.
- Or soak them in vinegar and water.

VANITY, PLASTIC LAMINATE OR PAINTED WOOD
- If a sponging with liquid detergent and water doesn't remove all the spots, use a gentle abrasive. (See also Laminate Countertops, p. 75.)

VINYL FLOORING
See p. 154.

WASTEBASKET
- *Wicker:* Scrub with warm, sudsy water, rinse thoroughly, air-dry.
- *Plastic:* Wipe with an all-purpose cleaner on a damp cloth. Rinse and dry. For stubborn stains, use a gentle abrasive.

WOODEN TOWEL RACKS, HOOKS, ETC., DULL
- Apply furniture polish. Buff.

NINE

The Bedroom

> ***Good enough housekeeping** is understanding that folding your sheets perfectly has nothing to do with how comfortable you'll feel in the bed.*

Isn't it weird how clothing that's just hanging in your closet can shrink a size or two for no apparent reason? If this has happened to any of your clothes, donate them to science (maybe someone can get to the bottom of this mystery) or give them to charity. The most important thing is to get them out of your house. Cleaning and reorganizing the closets is a major way to get your bedrooms in order.

Dejunk

PROBLEM: Night table surface cluttered with glasses, tissue, books, etc.

- Gather up all those creams, face masks, and any other stuff you need for night treatments and put them in a plastic shoe box (or a prettier container) that you can stow under the bed. Bonus: Your beauty secrets will be safe from casual snoops.

- Get a couple of cloth place mats that match your bedroom color scheme. Cut one in half vertically and hot-glue the half onto another whole one so that you have a pocket with a long flap. You can tuck the flap between the mattress and box spring. Now you've got a place to stow your personal stuff—and also the perfect place to hide the remote control from your channel-clicking spouse.

Control Freaking

Attach a beeper made to find car keys to the remote and you'll locate it wherever it is hiding—under the bed, behind the night table, between the couch cushions. (Of course, you may not want to find the darn thing.) My friend says that the real power battle in the bedroom is over the remote control. She gave her husband the shock of his life when he was clicking away one night and she suddenly produced a remote of her own and overrode his choice.

PROBLEM: Bedskirt slips and bunches, looks sloppy.

- Apply double-faced tape to the outer edges of the box spring, then place the skirt as usual.

- Or cut off the skirt, attach Velcro to it and a companion piece of Velcro to the innerspring mattress. It's easy to keep it in place, and when you want to launder it, you don't have to tear the whole bed apart.

When Velcro Gets Dusty

Velcro that's picked up lots of dirt doesn't attach as effectively. Clean it off by rubbing another piece of Velcro against it.

PROBLEM: No place to store blankets.
- Put them in zippered pillow covers and use them as throw pillows.
- Or lay them between the mattress and the box spring. They're safe from moths and available when needed.
- Or hang them on a curtain rod fastened to the back of the bedroom door. (In fact, add a second rod and use it to store the bedspread at night.)

Cover Up

An old zippered robe can be sewn up at the bottom, hung on a hanger, and used to hold quilts or other items that might discolor if stored in plastic. It's also a great hiding place for your valuables. (If you can't do the sewing, have your tailor do it for you.)

PROBLEM: Bed never neatly made.
- It's been proven that you get a better night's sleep if you get into a bed that's been made.
- Buy a blanket a size too small for the bed so it won't stick out under the comforter or spread.
- Fold the sheets in half vertically after you launder them and let the crease help you position the sheet exactly in the middle of the bed. Or put a tiny mark

with a laundry pen at the midpoint of the sheet to use as a gauge, so you won't be going from side to side, tugging and straightening.

• Don't keep your pillows in the shams. Instead, use the shams to hold extra blankets, linens, or nightclothes. You won't have to waste time stuffing the pillows back in every morning; just leave the filled shams in front of the pillows.

• Here's a trick for a child learning to make the bed. Sew some ribbon or rickrack as guidelines so that when it's lined up with the edges of the bed, just enough material will drape over the sides.

• Best of all: Go the duvet cover route. When you slip a duvet cover over your comforter, you don't need a top sheet. Just pull the duvet up in the morning and the bed's made in seconds. Yes, you have to wash the duvet cover as often as you would a sheet, but the protected comforter will need only infrequent washings. Be sure to choose a duvet cover that's lightweight and easy to wash.

Pull One Over

Here's how to slip the duvet cover on. Turn the cover inside out, slip your hands inside and reach to the bottom, then grab the duvet through the fabric. Don't let go, and pull your hands back out, shaking the cover down.

Allergy-proofing Your Home

I've put this in the Bedroom section because that's a good place to start.

• Use miteproof covers on pillows, mattress, and box springs.

• Use foam pillows and cotton blankets, never wool or down bedding.

• Wash bedding frequently in very hot water and dry it in the machine, since line drying attracts pollen.

• Keep windows closed and use air-conditioning when possible.

- Clean or replace filters in AC and heating systems regularly.
- Keep dust from circulating through the house by spraying the furnace filter with Endust. Or use fabric-softener sheets or pieces of nylon—or filters sold specifically for this purpose—under your floor registers. Slip them under the vents as air filters.
- Leave doors open to allow air to circulate through the house.
- Use a dehumidifier (and clean it often), because molds and dust mites thrive in dampness.
- Use a HEPA (high-efficiency particulate air) filter or a double bag in the vacuum to trap dust mites.
- Wear a mask while you dust and vacuum.
- Hang washable curtains rather than drapes.
- Leave floors bare or use area rugs rather than carpet.
- If you have a dog, bathe it as frequently as the vet recommends.
- Leave plants outdoors, since mold grows in soil.

PROBLEM: Shortage of storage room.
- Hampers, painted or covered, make night tables and storage space for linens, clothing, etc.
- Or transform a metal or plastic 40-gallon garbage pail into a storage unit/night table combination. Have a round plywood top made for it and cover it with a circular cloth that hangs all the way to the floor. A glass cover cut to size is inexpensive. Placed over the cloth, it will keep it clean and protect against spills.
- Recycle drawers from a cast-off bureau for storage; add casters to make them easy to roll. Or buy the plastic underbed storage units that come with built-in wheels. This is the perfect place for blankets, out-of-season clothes, and anything else you want to store.
- Clothes folded jelly-roll-style are more compact. Even shirts can be folded this way: Start by folding them in half lengthwise, then fold the sleeves over the shirt, and finally roll the shirt from the collar down.

Enough
^

Drawer Pull

- A drawer that's sticking may be damp. Put an extension cord into it with a lightbulb attached. (Place the bulb on a hot pad or other fireproof surface.) In a couple of hours, the light from the bulb should have dried it out.
- Or wave a hair dryer set on medium about 6 to 8 inches away from the problem spot.
- Or rub paraffin or paste wax or a candle stub along the bottom and sides of the drawer if it's wood, and give it a shot of silicone if it's metal.

PROBLEM: Closet is a mess.

- If you have a beat-up old wooden clothes rod, get a plastic shower curtain rod cover to snap over it—clothes will glide along and not bunch up.
- In case it actually occurs to someone to hang something up, be sure there's a hanger or hook available before the impulse passes. Buy lots of hangers and install hooks wherever you can.
- When you take something out of the closet, move its hanger to the front of the rod, so the hanger is ready for your use at the end of the day.
- It's amazing how color-coding the hangers helps keep things organized: Use one color for tops, another for bottoms; or, if you're sharing space with a spouse, each have your own hue.
- Also organize your closet by hanging like items in the same place. When you need a jacket, you shouldn't have to look through the entire closet to find one.
- This tip may appeal only to the truly compulsive who also happen to have wooden clothes poles. It definitely makes your closet look quite neat. File notches about an inch apart. Hangers will slip into them and clothes won't bunch together.

- Those hard-to-hang nighties and tops with spaghetti straps will stay where they're supposed to if you put a shower ring on a hanger, then hang the strappy item from it.
- Slip round shower rings over the clothing rod and you can slip several scarves on each. They may bunch, but that area most likely will be hidden by your hair.

How to Weed Out a Closet

It's been estimated that we wear 20 percent of our clothes 80 percent of the time. Unlike many statistics, this one makes sense to me, particularly if that other 80 percent consists mostly of clothes you're waiting to fit back into. When you do lose the weight, will those clothes still be in style? Get serious about clearing out stuff. Here's a helpful method for deciding what to salvage for yourself and what to salvage for the Salvation Army, other charity, or consignment shop.

- Ideally, you should take *all* your clothes into another room, then retrieve items as you need them. As you wear and launder clothing, return it to your bedroom closet, shelves, and dresser drawers. At the end of the season, you'll have figured out which clothes you are *really* wearing. Now take a good, hard look at the rest.
- Even if you don't have the luxury of an extra closet, you can manage a scaled-down version of this technique. Tie a ribbon at the front of the curtain rod, then return clothes in front of it as they're worn and washed. Clothes behind the ribbon are the ones that should go. Similarly, designate drawers and shelves as the "return" area for other types of clothing. A similar trick: Hang all hangers facing the same direction. Whenever you wear something, return it to the closet with the hanger facing the opposite way. Clothes hung in the original direction—the ones you clearly aren't wearing—are the ones that should go.

Enough
^

Clothes Quarters

- Double the hanging space by making a second tier in your closet; hang skirts and pants on the lower rod, shirts on the top one. (You may have to move the top rod higher to get sufficient clearance for two levels of clothing.) Here's how: Cut a thick-walled piece of PVC piping to the length of hanging space you'd like to add. Buy a piece of middleweight chain that's long enough to slip through the pipe with enough left over at each end to hang on to the top closet rod. Hang S hooks over the top rod and slip chains on. If removing hangers from the top rod is a problem, make a hooking tool by screwing a J-shaped metal wall hook into the top of a wooden broomstick.

- Get rid of those sliding doors (which are always coming out of the track, anyway) or the louver doors (which are a nuisance to clean), and get yourself more storage room at the same time. Replace them with frames and conventional doors, and then use the back of the door to hold shoe bags (use them for socks, panty hose, and more), a mirror, laundry bags, tie racks or hooks for your jewelry, clothes, etc.

- Now that shoulder pads are out of fashion, use them to make padded hangers by folding one over each end of the hanger and attaching it to itself with a safety pin. (When they come back into style, they'll be there for you.)

- Doubling (or tripling) up can save many inches of closet room. You don't need to buy one of the gadgets you see advertised on TV. Just buy S-shaped shower hooks and hang one around the neck of a hanger, then suspend another hanger from it. You don't have to stop at just one. Or use a length of chain suspended from a hanger, and slip another hanger through each link.

- Hang a metal S hook or a shower curtain hook from the clothes rod to hold your purses.

Shelf Game

- Have you considered doing away with your dresser and instead adding shelves inside the closet? For one thing, no dresser means no more dresser clutter. And you'll probably find it a lot easier to select a shirt or sweater from a stack than from a drawer where you can see only the one on top. (That's why they use shelves instead of dressers in clothing stores.)

- If you've got more closet space than shelf space, consider hanging what you'd normally put on a shelf: nightgowns, for example, can be slipped onto a hanger right out of the dryer, and they'll wrinkle less when hung.

- Instead of a drawer full of jumbled T-shirts, get yourself a shoe organizer meant to hang in a closet. Fold the T-shirts so the logos are visible and place two or three in each clear plastic loop so you can spot the one you want at a glance. These are also handy for storing sweat outfits.

- If you can't fit shelves into your closet, maybe you should build a closet for your shelves. Hang inexpensive laminated or warp-proof shelves on the wall, and have a carpenter frame a closet around them. You will need either plastic drawer units or plastic baskets for underwear, socks, and stockings—whether you'd prefer an open container or a closed one depends on your personal style. Either way, start your planning for this project by buying the drawer units or baskets first, then purchasing shelves that will accommodate them.

- Even within the baskets or drawers, you can subdivide. Put panty hose and socks of different colors into separate zipper-closing plastic bags; isolate rarely worn lingerie items into bags of their own.

- Is there a lot of air space left over the items on each shelf? You may be able to capture more storage room in the closet by installing more horizontal shelving. Besides, higher stacks of clothing are more likely to get sloppy. Build in conventional wooden shelves or

(continued)

Enough
∧

buy laminated shelving or rubber-coated wire shelving from a home center. (Cover those wire shelves with plastic rug runner—sold by the foot at home centers—if you want a solid surface.)

- Buy wire-coated metal "dividers"—they stand about 8 inches high—to slip onto shelves in between stacks of clothing to keep them from toppling over.

Your Right to Shoes

- Attach brackets to the back of the closet door about 8–10 inches from the floor, insert a curtain rod, and hang the heels of your shoes over it or your shoes behind it. Depending on the length of the rod and the number of shoes, you may need a center bracket for support.
- Liquor cartons come in many configurations, depending on the kind of bottle they hold. Some may be suitable as shoe cubbies. Spray-paint or cover with contact paper, if you choose.
- Shoes can also be stored on shelves, in boxes or not. If you're building a new closet, plan how many pairs of shoes you'll probably have—it's safe to assume at least as many as you have currently—and space the shelves accordingly.

DO'S for the Linen Closet

- Fold two sheets together, and when you put them away, fold the pillowcases in the middle. You'll have a neat little stackable bundle—and all the pieces will be together when it's time to change the linens.
- Fold and store seldom-used linens inside out. Dust won't show on the crease line. (Alternatively, put them over the rolled piece of cardboard that is on hangers the dry cleaner sends and hang them in a conventional closet.)
- Good enough: If you can't be bothered folding a fitted sheet neatly, fold it however you can, then slip it inside the pillowcase for neat stacking. If you're a little more persnickety about how your linens

look, learn the secret to folding a fitted sheet. Stretch your arms out, put one hand inside each of two corners of the sheet, then bring your hands together and "nest" one corner inside the other. Nest the other two, and finally nest one pair inside the other. Then lay the sheet on a flat surface and fold it smaller. Fold the top sheet neatly and fold this less-than-perfect bottom sheet inside. Sheets are pulled so taut on the bed that wrinkles won't be a problem.

- If comforters are too slippery to stack, slide them into empty pillowcases so you can stow them neatly in the closet.
- Or roll up blankets, comforters, and/or sleeping bags and secure them with an old belt or a bungee cord (sold in hardware or bicycle shops). They'll stay compactly rolled up and it'll be easy to grab on to the belt or elastic to pull them down.
- Add more horizontal shelves, closer together, if you need them.

Dejunking the Kids' Bedrooms

PROBLEM: Toys wall to wall.

- Cleaning is easier if you have clean dustpans on hand for scooping up Lego pieces or other little bitty items from all over the floor. Or use a rake to gather all the pieces together.
- Stuffed animals present a real storage problem. Attach Velcro patches to them and a matching square on the wall. Or sew hooks to each and hang them on one of those accordion-type racks with pegs.

- Or hang fishnet across two corners of the room and use this hammock to hold basketballs, soccer gear, etc. (It's also a fine tree house for those stuffed animals.)
- Your child's plastic swords, hockey sticks, and other long-handled toys can be put neatly into a round wastepaper basket or umbrella stand.
- A whole carton of empty shoe boxes from the local shoe store makes an interesting storage unit. Each box can hold a different item and can be slid out separately. Use for everything from rock and coin collections to a home for Barbie, her friends, and her possessions.

Too Much of a Good Thing

- At birthdays and Christmas, if your child has gotten heaps of new things, discreetly set aside a few. Bring them out at a later date, when others have been broken or discarded.
- I love this idea, passed on by a friend: In her house on Christmas Eve, next to the milk and cookies for Santa, the children set out toys he can pass on to other children.

PROBLEM: Clutter a constant issue.

- Buy office supply storage boxes, one per kid, and collect the school year's paper, artwork, and other memorabilia. As you and your child stow away this year's stuff, take the opportunity to go through last year's. Once time has passed, not every piece seems as precious, and you'll be able to toss some of it away.
- If space is really at a premium, have the kids curate an art show and hang their best works. Videotape the show and you won't have to keep the actual art. Well, maybe just a couple of pieces. . . .
- For extra storage in kids' rooms, buy used gym lock-

ers. Freshly painted, they not only store mitts, bats, helmets, skateboards, and toys, but also they look cute.

- Install hooks at kid height. If you make a neat row of them all along a brightly painted wall, they can hold everything from book bags to hats and actually look decorative.
- Install a Nerf basketball hoop over an open toy box and kids can have fun putting their toys away by tossing them into the hoop. (Big and little kids like this same trick over the washing machine.)
- What to do with those darn hats! Get an empty carpet roll from the carpet store, cover it with pretty contact paper or paint it, then fasten hooks at all heights, all around. (A stuffed toy collection could get the same treatment.)
- Resort to blackmail to get kids to cooperate. Pick up everything that's on the floor, hide it in a secret place, and charge a dime ransom per piece.
- If you have teenagers, throw in the towel. (They already have; it's lying on the floor.) Remind yourself they'll be out of the house soon.

Defend

THE BASIC SUPPLIES FOR GOOD ENOUGH BEDROOM CLEANING

> All-purpose cleaner or liquid detergent and cloth
> Dusting cloths
> Feather duster
> Glass cleaner
> Lambswool duster
> Vacuum cleaner

WEEKLY

TIDY UP AND AIR OUT.
- Put away any clothes that are lying around.

WHY: You can't clean surfaces that are covered with clutter.
- Open the windows.

WHY: Airing the room out helps prevent growth of mildew and bacteria.

MAKE UP THE BED.
- Change the sheets.

WHY: Because you know you should.

CLEAN THE MIRROR.
- Use glass cleaner as needed to spot-clean.

WHY: Prevent grime from building up.

CHECK WALLS, FURNITURE, AND WINDOWS.
- Spot-clean walls with heavy-duty cleaners if needed.
- Go over dusty furniture with a slightly damp cloth, wipe dry.

- Spray light-duty cleaner on cloth, wipe obviously dirty windows clean.

WHY: Prevent grime from building up.

DUST BLINDS, LAMPSHADES, LIGHTBULBS, PICTURES, FURNITURE, WINDOWSILLS.

- Use your feather duster and lambswool duster. See Dusting 101, p. 35.

WHY: Prevent layers of dust from accumulating.

VACUUM FLOOR.

- Go over high-traffic areas after you've dusted.

WHY: Prevent dirt from being ground into the floor or carpet.

EVERY **3** MONTHS

Memory Jogger

Schedule jobs that should be done twice or four times a year or so—turning the mattress, cleaning the ceiling fan, checking the batteries in the smoke alarms—to coordinate with the change of clocks or the change of seasons: June 21, September 21, etc. It's easier to remember them.

CLEAN THE CEILING FAN.

- Usually manufacturers recommend cleaning every 2–3 months. Be sure to turn off the power before you start.
- Buy the special tool that attaches to an extension pole for cleaning ceiling fans (it slips over the blade). Or do it by hand: Climb up on a ladder, slip your hand into an old sock, and dip your hand into a solution of water with a little bit of soap. Slide your hand over the top and bottom of one blade, then over onto the next.
- If your fan has brass or metal blades, it may need a special cleaner. Some folks apply a layer of floor wax, but to me that just seems like a lot of extra work.

Enough
^

WHY: An accumulation of dust may interfere with the smooth operation of the fan.

TURN THE MATTRESS.

- If you can't remember which end should be up (I can relate to that!), use a marking pen and mark the head of one side 1, the foot 2, and the head and foot of the other side 3 and 4. (As you turn the mattress, you'll probably notice a little dust between the bed and the wall. Now's the time to run the vacuum on these "hidden" areas.)

WHY: Sleeping in the same spot, you wear out the mattress.

Drawer Pull
If your dresser is too heavy to move, you can still vacuum underneath to get out dustballs and clean out places where insects might like to nest. Just pull out the bottom drawer(s) and you'll have a space for the vacuum hose to reach into.

VACUUM CLOSETS AND DRAWERS.

WHY: Dust at the bottom of the closet or in the niches of drawers is a great breeding ground for moths and carpet beetles, which will make a smorgasbord of your wardrobe.

Stocking Cap
You don't have to empty out your drawers to vacuum them out. Just pull a leg of your panty hose over the vacuum hose or the nose of the cordless vacuum so the machine won't suck up any jewelry or other small items.

EVERY 6 MONTHS
WASH THE CURTAINS.

WHY: If they get very dingy, you can't get them clean again.

CLEAN THE ENTIRE RUG.

- Pull out heavy furniture to vacuum underneath. If you don't have sliders under the legs, slip a paper bag under each and it'll move out easily. To vacuum the whole rug, divide it into sections and do one "row" at a time.

WHY: Prevent ground-in dirt.

WASH THE BEDDING.

- Wash mattress pad, pillow covers, bed skirts.
- Put pillows into wash or into dryer on no-heat cycle. (Coordinate this with turning the mattress.)

WHY: A little dust may be okay, but a lot of dust will build up into grime and may aggravate allergies.

Decide

BLANKETS

- *Electric:* Follow care instructions on the label. Most electric blankets are designed for laundering, usually in cold or lukewarm water. Let them soak for about 10 minutes and then put them on a short cycle to reduce the amount of pilling. Line-dry unless the manufacturer specifies that machine drying at a low temperature is okay. Wiring may be damaged if electric blankets are dry-cleaned or cleaned with solvents.
- *Wool:* Check the care label; not all can be machine-washed. Make sure the machine is big enough so that the blanket can move around enough to get clean. If

your home machine doesn't have the capacity, go to the Laundromat or you risk tearing the blanket.

BRASS BED

• Usually lacquered. To clean, just wipe it down with a damp cloth. But if the lacquer's peeling, you (or a pro) will have to remove the lacquer, then recoat. Your hardware store can recommend products.

COMFORTERS

• In most cases, these can be washed and dried by machine (see below), but don't try doing them at home if your machine doesn't have a large capacity. You might damage them or tear the fabric. Go to a commercial Laundromat instead.

• Down comforters, say some manufacturers, should be professionally cleaned, but I've been washing them in my machine, on gentle, for years. Use a soap made for down or a low-sudsing detergent such as Ivory Snow, since too much soap removes the oil from down. You may need to keep the comforter in the dryer for 3 hours at a moderate temperature (and be careful, because commercial machines get hot enough to burn these items).

• Synthetic or Dacron-filled comforters can generally be machine-washed (check the care label). Add detergent to machine, soak for 10 minutes, then wash on a short, gentle cycle. Check care label for drying instructions.

• Older comforters and quilts may fall apart if you don't mend small rips or tears before you put them in the machine. Use duct tape for a temporary fix if you can't be bothered sewing.

CURTAINS

• *Dusty:* Occasional vacuuming helps avoid built-up dirt. When you use the dusting tool, make sure your vacuum is turned to low suction. If the sheers are pulled into the machine, they may rip. See suction control adjustment information in Dusting 101, p. 35.

• *Soiled:* Always check manufacturer's recommendations. Curtains are prone to water stains (which can be removed only by water), but since such stains come from a leak and contain grime from an unknown source, they may be tricky to remove. Take the curtains down, marking lightly with a pen to indicate where hooks should be placed, and read the care instructions before you throw them in the machine. Don't jam them into the washer because that will create extra wrinkles. Rinse thoroughly, since soap attracts dust; use fabric softener to minimize creasing; and hang them immediately so creases can fall out. It will also help if you spray them lightly with spray starch and/or push a dowel through the bottom hem so the weight helps pull out wrinkles.

• Fiberglass curtains can't be machine-washed or -dried because the glass fragments break. Hand-wash them in the tub in soapy water, swishing them around, then rinse them in cool, clear water. Don't wring them. Just hang them and let them air-dry. Handle with care, and rinse out the tub to remove any fragments left behind.

• Lined curtains must be dry-cleaned by professionals.

Rod Steward

To prevent curtains from snagging when you put them back on the rod, coat the rod tip with clear nail polish, cover it with a small plastic bag, or wrap with a bit of masking tape.

DRAPES

See p. 163 and p. 175.

HARDWARE ON ANTIQUE FURNITURE

- Usually made of brass. Using a commercial cleaner may make the brass look too new. Instead, rub it with 0000 steel wool to remove some of the tarnish but not all of the patina. Be gentle: Some "brass" is only a thin coating.

IRON BED

- *Unpainted:* Most good quality "iron" beds today are actually steel. Wipe with a damp cloth and remove any visible grime with some mild liquid dish detergent and water. Abrasives and polishes may scratch the finish.
- *Painted finish:* Check with the manufacturer regarding care.
- *Peeling:* If you're feeling crafty, use a commercial paint stripper, then sand the rough spot, cover it with rust-preventing primer, and follow up with a coat of paint. But if you asked me, I'd say you were lucky, and leave it. The "distressed" look is very popular today. (CAUTION: If you suspect it may have been painted with lead-based paint, you need a pro to deal with it.)

LAMPS AND LAMPSHADES

See p. 182.

LOUVER DOORS

- When the dust is thick enough to notice, wrap a cloth around a ruler, a spatula, or an 8-inch drywaller's blade, spray it with a mist of water, and run it across each louver. You can slip it between the slats and work it up and around, cleaning each slat thoroughly.

MATTRESSES

- My favorite device for cleaning up mattresses is Bissell Little Green Machine, the water extraction cleaner that

I recommend for use with wet spills. But if you don't have one, here are some alternative suggestions.

- *Urine:* Blot up liquid with rags, pressing hard against the spot to absorb as much as possible, then lay weights on top of towels on the spot for several hours if possible. Apply a commercial carpet stain remover as directed by the product label. Stand the mattress on its side to prevent moisture from getting deeper inside and wait until it's dry. Then lay the mattress flat, apply a layer of baking soda or cat box filler, and leave overnight. Or dampen and rub borax into the areas and let dry. Brush or vacuum to remove the dry borax. Or check pet stores for products such as Nature's Miracle and Simple Solution; use as directed.
- *Musty:* Use a commercial foam upholstery cleaner, following instructions. Or use Febreze odor remover.
- *Stained:* Upholstery shampoo can remove mattress stains. Follow instructions. Excessive liquid may cause mildewing.

ODOR IN CLOSET OR DRAWERS

- Calcium carbonate crystals, activated charcoal, or baking soda in an open container help keep down odors and musty scents. Or use a high-quality odor remover such as Nilium that eats scents and doesn't just mask them.
- *Home remedies for drawers:* Fill them with crumpled newspaper, one or two charcoal briquettes or a sheet or two of fabric softener, and seal drawers tightly for a few days.
- *Home remedies in the closet:* Punch holes in a one-pound coffee can, fill with charcoal briquettes, cover, and place on the floor. (Use a three-pound can for larger closets.) Or fill the leg of an old pair of panty hose with cedar chips (pet stores have them), tie a knot, and hang it inside the closet to make it smell

better. But don't make the mistake of thinking this will repel moths. Only mothballs and flakes will do that job.

- If a room needs extra freshening power, I've heard good things about a battery-operated wall mounted machine that releases a shot of freshener into the air every 15 minutes. (You've seen them in hospitals.)

- Mildew can do great damage to your clothes. (See below.) If you suspect that persistent odors indicate the presence of mold, see Mold Story, p. 74.

Preventing Mildew in the Clothes Closet

- To keep closets warm and dry, keep a low-watt bulb burning all the time (but safely away from anything that might catch fire). A new plug-in device releases warm air; this is perfect for very humid situations.
- Don't leave damp clothing in the closet.
- Clean items before you store them.
- Use a moth control product that contains paradichlorobenzene; it also inhibits mildew.
- There's a product called DampRid containing calcium chloride that is made to be hung in a closet or any other damp spot to absorb moisture. Other chemicals, such as silica gel and activated alumina, can be used to absorb moisture from the area. If you can't find these in your home center, try a scientific supply house or call your local university extension center, and put some in bags to hang in the closet.

PICTURES
See p. 184.

PILLOW COVERS

- Their purpose is to keep the pillow itself protected from oils and perspiration. They're machine washable but will eventually get too stained to clean and must be discarded. Once upon a time, all pillow covers were thick, which made them truly protective, but in recent years, you haven't been able to get any but thin ones. (This is one of those few cases where "thin" is *not* better.) Look for the ones that are quilted like a mattress pad; they're the only kind that makes sense.

PILLOWS

- Always check care instructions on the label to see whether a pillow can be washed. If you wash a pillow, it is essential to dry it thoroughly. This may require as much as a 3-hour spin in the dryer. Drying two at once will keep the load balanced, and putting a clean tennis ball or tennis shoe covered with a sock in the machine will keep the pillows fluffed up. Set the control to medium high and watch carefully so they don't burn. Pillows that aren't properly dry may mildew, in which case they'll never regain their loft. What's worse, they'll smell.
- Pillows filled with kapok are unwashable.
- Polyester pillows are usually machine washable and dryable.
- To clean feather and down pillows, use cool water and a low-sudsing detergent such as Ivory Snow, since too much soap removes oil from down. Agitate only 4–8 minutes on regular cycle. Use three rinses. Machine-dry, following instructions above.
- Foam pillows should be hand-washed in mild detergent unless the label advises otherwise, then rolled in a towel with excess water squeezed out. Foam must be air-dried since in an electric dryer they might cause a fire. Drying will take two days or more.
- Oversized pillows should be taken to a large-capacity machine at a Laundromat to ensure they're thoroughly washed and rinsed, then thoroughly dried.

Enough
∧

Radiator Cleanup

Here's a great way to tackle a messy job. Cover a very dusty radiator with an old, damp sheet. Using a vacuum cleaner with a blower attachment, insert the long crevice tool under the sheet and between each fin of the radiator to blow dirt onto the sheet. Leave the sheet in place until the dust settles, then remove and launder it, and sweep up any excess dirt.

STUFFED TOYS

- Plush nylon toys or those marked "all-new materials" may be machine-washed on cold/gentle. (To prepare for machine handling, cover "hair" with an old stocking and tie it closed before putting the item in the machine.) Rinse on gentle, put in the dryer on air only for one or two cycles, and if the toys are still damp, put them somewhere where they can continue to dry out for as long as necessary.
- Unwashable toys may look cleaner if you rub them with dry cornstarch. Let it stand briefly, then brush it off. You can also freshen them by giving them a spin in the clothes dryer set to air only (prepare for machine handling as above).
- For a stubborn stain on unwashable items, shake some liquid detergent with water in a covered bowl until you get foam. Dip a dry brush into the foam and spot-clean the item, one small spot at a time. Blot off excess moisture with a clean, dry towel. Air-dry for 1–2 days, then "fluff" with a dry hairbrush, brushing first in one direction, then the other. If the toy's owner is young enough to put toys in his or her mouth, don't use harsh cleaners. Otherwise, an upholstery cleaner may be of some help.

Allergy Reliever

If dust mites are a problem, one way to help is to put a stuffed animal in a plastic bag and pop it in the freezer overnight. Allow it to defrost before returning it to the child. Freezing will kill the mites.

WALLPAPER

- Most contemporary wallpapers are made of vinyl, which is designed to be washed. But if you're not sure whether the paper is water sensitive, test in a small, inconspicuous place before you do anything. Use the gentlest solution first—liquid detergent and water—and use a paper towel or soft cloth as a scrubber.

  If the paper doesn't fade, run, or bleed and doesn't seem otherwise damaged, use the detergent on the problem spot. Apply as little liquid as possible and work from the outside of the spot in. Rinse with a clean sponge dipped in cool water. If the detergent doesn't remove the dirt, try glass cleaner and a very gentle scrubber.
- If the paper is unwashable, use an artgum eraser or kneadable dough to clean off spots.

The Writing on the Wall

I always say that the writing on the wall is not a sign that something bad is going to happen—it already did. If stain removal for painted walls (see p. 156) doesn't really cover up handprints or other surface blemishes, work with the problem. Buy colored paint, dip in your hands and your kids', and press them to the wall to make a fun pattern. Or buy paint a couple of shades darker than the original wall and try sponge-painting it.

WATERBED MATTRESS

- Wipe it down with ½ cup baking soda in 1 quart of water. (I personally think these things aren't worth the trouble.)

TEN

The Kitchen

> **Good enough housekeeping** is using
> the good silver every day so you never
> have to polish away the tarnish.

A friend of mine is affected by a weird, though very real, syndrome that causes her to wake up, get out of bed, and sleepwalk into the kitchen. While sound asleep, and without any awareness of it, she raids the refrigerator in the middle of the night. She discovered this only when she found evidence each morning—dirty dishes, half-eaten food—and there was no one else home to blame it on. Imagine if she could tap such energy in better ways! Wouldn't it be great to clean the house while asleep and unconscious?

Dejunk

PROBLEM: Not enough cabinet space.

- Make that useless cabinet above the refrigerator functional. Remove the doors, install vertical wood dividers, and now you've got a place to store your trays, cutting boards, and cookie sheets.
- Don't ignore the insides of the cabinet doors. They can hold lid holders and narrow shelves—along with hooks for pot holders, corkboard for messages, and more.
- As I mentioned in the introduction, if you have certain tools that you use only at certain times—the lamb cake mold for Easter, the cookie press for Christmas cookies, the barbecue tools for summer months—they can be packed away until needed, staying dust-free and relieving some of the clutter.

Door Holder

If kitchen cabinet doors don't stay shut, use Velcro to solve the problem—one piece on the door, a companion piece on the frame.

PROBLEM: Not enough counter space.

- Measure the total shelf space your spice collection takes up and put up Velcro (self-stick, stapled, or nailed) in the appropriate length(s) below your cabinets. Then attach 1-inch squares of the companion pieces to your spice containers.
- Or buy a length of magnetic tape from the craft store, peel the sticky tape off the back, and press it high on

Enough
∧

the back wall of the kitchen cabinet—above the level of the other items. Attach metal spice cans to the strip.

- Those clunky knife blocks take up a lot of room and rarely hold all your knives. A magnetic bar mounted on a wall is much more efficient and holds other metal items too—potato peeler, can opener, long spoons and forks.

- Your pegboard can hold more than tools. You can hang sturdy shelves on it, and they in turn can hold cookbooks, the toaster oven, coffee grinder, and other small appliances.

- Put a horizontal row of hooks along a suitable wall and use them for hanging anything from tools to a string of garlic.

- Under-cabinet appliances (and even radios) are made to solve the counter-space problem. So are plastic drawer units. Check out the possibilities.

PROBLEM: Equipment is disorganized.
- Devote one drawer exclusively to the implements you use all the time: spatula, tongs, slotted spoon, measuring spoon, peeler, paring knife. You won't have to rummage through a ton of stuff for what you need.

- In the prop department of a theater company, I saw an idea to adapt to the kitchen. The tools were hung on a pegboard, and the silhouette of each was painted on the board so you knew just what belonged where. It's a lot of work up front, but it pays off in the end because everything stays in its place.

- Put what you need where you need it: The silverware and dishes should be stored next to the dishwasher, for rapid emptying, or near the table, convenient to setting.

DO'S in a Kitchen if You're Planning to Remodel

- Have a swing-arm faucet installed near the stove. You can fill up the teapot or big pots of water for cooking pasta without lugging them across the room. For the same reason, install a drain near the stove.
- Consider installing a second dishwasher. It's often cheaper than conventional cabinetry and very useful in a busy household. And you never have to unload. Items go from dishwasher to table.
- Sealed burners on the stove top mean no mess from boilovers.
- Under counters, replace shelves with drawers wherever possible. If items in the back are easy to reach, you have much more usable storage space.
- Build cabinets clear up to the ceiling. You can use the extra storage, and the open area just collects dust.
- Buy appliances that have the fewest knobs and gadgets—less to clean. (Also less to go wrong. Someone could make a fortune marketing appliances with only two options: On and off.)
- Rubber-covered wire shelving or other storage devices inside your freezer and/or fridge make everything more convenient to reach.
- Go for the lowest-maintenance surfaces you can: Corian or similar solid surface synthetic for counters, Pergo wood laminate for floors. They're easy to care for and practically indestructible.
- If you've simply got to have stone, choose granite (or slate or sandstone) for the kitchen and leave marble for the bath, foyer, or fireplace. Marble is softer than other stones and even when it's sealed is more vulnerable to scratches and stains. Granite, slate, and sandstone (siliceous stones) can be cleaned with mild acids like vinegar, while marble and limestone (calcareous stones) cannot.
- And if you're tiling, use dark or neutral grouting on the floor and especially on counters, where it's most likely to become stained during the preparation of food.

DON'TS in a Kitchen

- Avoid high-maintenance surfaces like butcher block if you like everything to look perfect.
- Also avoid glass-windowed cabinets or even translucent ones. In the showroom they look great, but that's because in the showroom the cereal boxes are all the same height and the stacks of dishes are perfectly matched, so the view behind the doors is always attractive.
- Avoid textured surfaces, which are always harder to clean than smooth surfaces. One fancy store showed tiles textured like a tin roof in the backsplash area—a cleaning nightmare. Raised areas or indents in a floor are problematic, too.

To do . . .

Defend

THE BASIC SUPPLIES FOR GOOD ENOUGH KITCHEN CLEANING

All-purpose cleaners, light and heavy-duty
Abrasive cleaner
Broom and/or vacuum
Bucket
Dishcloths
Glass cleaner
Lambswool duster
Oven cleaner
Rubber gloves
Rubbing alcohol

Single-edged razor blades
Sponges/scouring pads
Wiping cloth or paper towels

DAILY
NEATEN UP.
- Put away everything that's out of place, including dishes (put in cupboards or dishwasher) and dish towels (put them in laundry if necessary); close cabinet doors.

WHY: The less clutter, the less dirt and the faster the cleanup.

QUICK-CLEAN COUNTERTOPS AND SURFACES OF APPLIANCES.
- Use all-purpose spray cleaner on all materials, including acrylic, ceramic tile (glazed and unglazed), stainless steel, cultured marble, and plastic laminate. Let set briefly, then wipe with dishcloth or sponge.
- For a stubborn spot, try degreasing cleaner. Or apply a paste of baking soda and water, let it set half an hour, then try again. Or use a scraping tool. A single-edge razor will surely do the job. Just be sure to keep the surface wet so it doesn't scratch.

WHY: Stains left on countertops or appliances may leave permanent discoloration, if left on cooktop or front of range may bake on. It's much easier to clean up a fresh stain than a stain that's had time to set in.

STERILIZE THE SPONGE.
- ✿ Microwave the sponge and/or dishcloth for 30 seconds or run it through the dishwasher. Make sure the cloth is secured in the dishwasher. (A clothespin will do the job.)

WHY: The most bacteria-infested spot in the house, according to some studies, is the inside of a sponge. Microwaving banishes germs and also gets rid of odor.

Enough
^

EMPTY THE GARBAGE PAILS.

WHY: Full pails are unsanitary and may create unpleasant odors. If someone's looking for a great Christmas present idea, drop a hint that you'd like a trash compactor. (It gets daily use, unlike the negligee.)

21 Ways to Save Kitchen Cleanup Time

1. Large coffee filters are useful for lining your steamer basket. They're strong enough to lift out cooked food, and there's no cleanup. Use them also to line the measuring cup of your diet scale.

2. Prevent splattering from an electric mixer by cutting a hole in the middle of a paper plate and putting the mixer's beaters through it.

3. Always mix food in extra-large bowls so nothing goes over the sides.

4. Cook food that will splatter in a deep pot, like a Dutch oven, rather than in a fry pan.

5. Or turn a colander—the kind with pinholes—upside down over the frying pan. The air gets in, but the grease is contained.

6. And cover the other burners with a cookie sheet when you're frying. It's much easier to wash the single cookie sheet than all the other burners and the surface of the cooktop.

7. Or buy burner covers that offer protection and look nice, too.

8. Line drip pans and reflector bowls with foil or replace them with new ones that are black and nonstick.

9. When grating cheese or bread crumbs, place the grater inside a plastic bag as you work and you won't have to wipe up the counter.

10. Use spoon rests so you won't have to keep wiping off the counter.

11. Measure anything that is likely to spill over the sink; or open the dishwasher and measure it over the door. Do likewise when you have to give anything a coat of nonstick spray or perform any other messy jobs. Again, no counter cleanup.

12. You're not supposed to wash a flour sifter (because the wet flour will turn into paste), but you can prevent it from leaking flour on the cupboard shelf by slipping a plastic top from a coffee can over the bottom. (Margarine tub lids fit smaller sifters.)

13. Put oven-cooked foods in a pan deep enough so there won't be any spillover. But just in case, line the bottom of the oven with foil to catch drips.

14. Line the inside of pans that aren't nonstick with foil when you're baking; you have no problem with cookies or cakes sticking to the pan, and cleanup is as quick as tossing out the foil.

15. Keep a colander in the sink and scrape scraps from the dishes into it. It's a lot easier (and more pleasant) than bending over the pail. Also, liquids will go down the drain and not into the garbage pail, where they create odor and another cleanup job.

16. Baking pans and other metal cookware are less likely to rust if you dry them thoroughly. Put a coffee filter inside to absorb moisture as an extra precaution.

17. Make sure the undersides of all appliances have pads, or buy and affix felt pads, so they don't scratch laminates. If you want to be extra-careful, apply a coat of a light furniture wax (even car or floor wax) to the laminates to help them resist stains and scratches.

18. Spray the bowl with nonstick spray before you serve your pet. You won't have to spend time scraping off dried-on food.

19. Cover hard-to-reach areas such as the tops of kitchen cabinets or the refrigerator with sheets of waxed paper. It's easier to strip off the old paper and replace it with new than to climb a ladder with a bucketful of soapy water and start scrubbing.

20. When you're broiling, put a bit of water under the broiling rack in the pan beneath it to collect smoke and grease and make cleanup easier. Or place a slice of bread underneath the rack to blot grease.

21. Turn on the ventilating fan whenever you're cooking, not just when there's smoke. It draws up grease that would otherwise be deposited on walls and other surfaces.

TWICE A WEEK
SPOT-CLEAN GLASS, PLASTIC, AND CHROME.

- Give a shot of glass cleaner to all surfaces where there are fingerprints or smudges. After spraying, use a wip-

Enough
∧

ing cloth in one hand to wipe off dirt, cloth in the other hand to dry it.

WHY: To prevent dirt buildup. The more layers of dirt on any surface, the harder it is to clean.

DEGREASE DOOR HANDLES, CABINETS, WALL BEHIND SINK, KNOBS, DRAWER PULLS.

- Use all-purpose heavy-duty spray cleaner on spots and smudges or obvious grease spots on walls, fridge, range, front of oven, top of fridge. After spraying, hold one clean cloth in each hand. Use one to wipe off dirt, the other hand to dry the area.

WHY: To prevent dirt buildup.

When You're Seeing Spots

If the dishwasher isn't doing its usual good job, before you call the technician, check for bits of paper, toothpicks, plastic wrap, glass, etc., that may be clogging the small holes in the spray arm(s) or any other area.

WEEKLY
CLEAN THE FLOOR.

- Sweep or vacuum up dirt. (You're advised to use the floor nozzle tool on the vacuum so as not to damage the floor and the machine, but I've used my regular vacuum beater bar on kitchen floors for years without any problem. If you want to, do this at your own risk.)
- To clean the baseboards, use your lambswool duster (or just wear socks and run your foot along the area).
- Then mop. See Base Hits, next page.

WHY: Whatever is dropped on the floor may be ground in and cause damage; also, crumbs attract insects.

Base Hits

Simply cleaning your baseboard is the good enough solution, but if you want to touch up your wooden baseboard, use lemon oil on light woods and Old English Scratch Cover in the original finish or the red finish, whichever matches your decor, on dark woods.

How to Mop

- *Nonwood floors:* If you have a Sh-Mop, dampen it and wring it out, then squirt a vinegar water mixture (3 tablespoons vinegar to 1 quart water) onto the floor, and mop. If the Sh-Mop becomes very dirty, rinse it and continue. If you are using a conventional mop or if the cleaning solution leaves a film, you may need to go over the floor with clean water.
- *Wood floors:* Use very little water. Even surface-sealed wood floors may have spaces between planks or cracks in the finish, and if water seeps into them, it may cause staining or damage. Mist your mop lightly with water or use Swiffer wet wipes. Or wrap a dampened cloth around your mop, replacing it with a clean one as it gets dirty. Don't use ammonia; it will dull the surface.

CHECK THE REFRIGERATOR.

- Throw out old food and wipe up any spills.

EVERY FEW WEEKS

OIL BUTCHER BLOCK COUNTERTOP.

- Whether or not you actually plan to use the butcher block for chopping (and I wouldn't use it for meat, fish, or poultry; refer to Making the Cut, p. 125), it needs regular maintenance. First clean it by mixing ½ cup baking soda with a quart of warm water, use a good steel scraper or spatula, rinse with water, and blot dry. Never use harsh detergents or a steel brush, which may gouge. Then rub mineral oil or whatever other oil the manufacturer suggests (but not food oils, which get rancid) and wipe away the excess.

WHY: Butcher block that's dry will eventually split.

CLEAR THE DRAINS.

- ✿ Boil a gallon of water, then pour half into the drain, wait a minute or so, then pour in the other half.

WHY: This will help prevent clogs. See p. 134.

Drain Solution

Bacterial drain cleaners are sold through catalogs that offer products that benefit the environment as well as in hardware and grocery stores. Many use a combination of enzymes to break down food, grease, and organic waste, but what really makes these cleaners so effective are the helpful bacteria that colonize your drain and live off this waste material. It takes a while for the bacteria to become established, and most treatments require several applications plus monthly maintenance, because bacteria are constantly being washed away by whatever goes down your drain. This solution won't harm your pipes or the environment and is recommended if you have frequent clogs.

OCCASIONALLY
CLEAN THE RANGE HOOD.

- ✿ *Fastest:* Cover the burners on the stove below with towels. Spray on a degreaser such as Simple Green, and let the grime drip down onto the towels. Use a damp cloth to give the hood a final wipe.
- Charcoal filters cannot be washed but must occasionally be replaced.
- Mesh filters should be washed periodically in hot soapy water or in the dishwasher, or replaced. Your manual will advise how often this should be done.
- The filter cover can be washed in hot soapy water or

the dishwasher. It should be dried completely before it is put back in place.
- Clean the bulb when cool with a damp cloth.

WHY: Greasy buildup and clogged filters can restrict air flow and cause motor overheating, which may damage the motor and is a fire hazard.

CLEAN UNDER AND BEHIND THE REFRIGERATOR.

- Cover a yardstick with an old sock and slip it underneath.
- Or just before tossing a bathmat or braided rug into the wash, slide it under the refrigerator to pick up dust and dirt.
- Or use the cardboard roll from inside gift wrap and slip it over your vacuum hose.
- Or buy a coil-cleaning brush made expressly for this purpose.

WHY: Refrigerator coils must be exposed to the air. If they're coated with a layer of dirt, heat gets trapped inside and the refrigerator won't cool properly. If they're clean, they use less electricity, operate more efficiently, and last longer. Most coils are cunningly hidden either on the rear of the fridge or behind a panel at the front bottom so that you can stay blissfully unaware that they're filthy until your electric bills rise or your refrigerator conks out.

- If there's a space between refrigerator and the cabinetry, this is a good time to clean it out. Attach a nylon scrubber to a yardstick, dip it into detergent, push it in, pull out dust. Rinse off the scrubber and repeat until it comes out clean.

Enough
       Λ

Moving Experience

To move a heavy appliance like the fridge away from the wall without scratching the floor, use one of the following methods.

- Spray the floor in front of the item (and legs if it has any) with Windex.
- Or soap the floor.
- Or set the two front legs or weight-bearing spots on a towel, glossy magazine, or anything else that will slide, even carpet tiles. (If you use the carpet tiles, turn them foam side up. Foam will keep appliance from slipping, carpet will slide over floors.)
- Or use the disks to put under heavy furniture sold for this purpose.
- Or get your teenager to slide a skateboard underneath it.
- And if there's no place to grip, buckle several heavy leather belts together and slip them over an end or corner. Or use a bungee cord.

WHY: When you pull it out and see what's there, you'll know.

DECLARE A TOSS-OUT DAY FOR YOUR REFRIGERATOR.

- Discard that bottle of barbecue sauce you used for the Fourth of July 1999 and the chutney leftover from your Millennium New Year's Eve party. And even if you toss out only the dried-out mustards, you'll probably have some mustard left. Check the expiration date on the horseradish, lemon juice, salad dressings, etc.

WHY: Reduce the risk of food poisoning, and clear space for the new assortment of sauces, mustards, dressings, and other items that you will throw away next year. . . .

MY READERS TIP ME OFF: Waxing Appliances

To some, it might seem like just too much work to apply appliance or light furniture wax (even car or floor wax) to plastic laminate counters, appliances, and/or cabinets. But some of my readers and TV viewers insist it's worth the trouble: The wax makes it easy to wipe clean, helps resist stains, keeps painted surfaces brighter, makes surfaces more scratch-resistant.

Decide

ALUMINUM COOKWARE, SCORCHES ON

- ✪ If the interior is discolored, acidic foods may remove stains as they are cooking. For a stubborn stain, fill pot with water and add 2–3 tablespoons of vinegar or 2 teaspoons of cream of tartar to each quart of water, then boil; or boil some lemon or apple peel with water; then rinse and dry.
- CAUTION: Cooking acidic foods or foods made with milk or eggs in aluminum pots may pit the pots permanently unless you rinse them out immediately after cooking. Bleach may cause discoloration too.

For Squeaky Wheels

To lubricate blenders, egg beaters, and any other kitchen appliance with movable parts, use mineral oil. Unlike salad oil, mineral oil is noncorrosive and won't turn rancid. As with salad oil, if a little lands on your food it won't cause a problem.

BLINDS, GREASY

- Close them, then wipe with all-purpose cleaner.
- Or clean them with ammonia and water if they're extremely dirty. Rinse with a clean cloth dipped into hot water. See Blinds, pp. 168–169.
- Keep them up more than down and they'll stay cleaner.

Handy Ideas

- To get the smell of onion, garlic, or fish off your hands, rub them with coffee grounds, toothpaste, or vinegar; or add a little salt to the soap.
- The weirdest remedy (and it works instantly): Place all five fingers on the handle of a stainless steel spoon and run cold water over them.

BRASS FIXTURES

- *Dirt on lacquered fixtures:* Wipe with damp, wet cloth.
- *Tarnish on unlacquered fixtures:* Use a brass polish. Or rub gently with a paste of salt and lemon juice or ammonia. Wash, rinse, and dry.

BURNER PANS

- ✪ *Food burned on:* To clean the metal rings around the burners, fill the sink with hot water and a cup of ammonia. Let the rings soak overnight, and by morning you should be able to rub them clean with a plastic scrubber. Or sprinkle Biz over each, let set, then rinse. If they're badly soiled, just replace them.
- *Plastic melted on:* Use a hair dryer to heat the melted plastic. Hold it 6–8 inches away, waving back and forth. Use a scraper to scrape away residue while it's still warm.

BUTCHER BLOCK

- Staining, warping, and separating will occur if brine, water, and/or blood all are allowed to stand on the surface. To remove stain, use a very fine sandpaper (such as 220) or fine dry steel wool (grade 0000), rub with the grain, then re-oil with mineral oil.

- Or scrub with ¼ cup bleach in a quart of warm water, rub with a lemon; or cover with bleach and salt, scrub with a stiff (but not metal) brush; then wash with very hot, soapy water and wipe dry with a clean cloth.
- Remove gummy dough on a wood board by sprinkling salt on a wet sponge and start rubbing. Or use a plastic windshield scraper. It won't mark the wood.

Making the Cut

There's been a lot of controversy about whether plastic or wood cutting boards are safer. The solution that makes the most sense to me is buying three plastic ones and color coding them for use—one for poultry, one for meat and fish, one for fruits and vegetables. (You can even buy a set of flexible plastic cutting sheets in four different colors.) Poultry needs to be cooked at the highest temperature and is the most likely to carry bacteria, which is why it's separate from other meat and also fish; fruits and vegetables are the lowest risk. Wash all boards in the dishwasher to be safe, though wooden ones will eventually split, and have to be replaced.

Shelf Solutions

- Laminate shelves can be wiped with all-purpose cleaner.
- *Good enough:* Give wood shelves a coating of polyurethane so you can dispense with lining and just wipe them clean.
- Rubber shelf lining can be cut to size and slipped into the dishwasher when grimy.
- Stick-on lining is durable, but if it's getting shabby and you need to peel it off, wave a hair dryer over it to loosen the glue and peel it up. WD-40 can help loosen stubborn spots. Alternative: Cover it with another layer of paper.
- Ribbed plastic shelf covering that comes in a roll is excellent for under glasses. But it's not good in a kitchen in areas where the air is sooty or dirty, or on a low shelf where dust is likely to accumulate. When ribbing gets soiled, dirt gets trapped in the ridges. It

(continued)

can't simply be wiped clean but must be taken out and scrubbed or put in the dishwasher.

- At home centers, you can buy vinyl flooring in short lengths (sometimes as remnants). You can trim it to fit your shelf—if necessary, put it in the sun so it will be very pliable—and it makes a great lining. It's available in a variety of colors and patterns, durable, and easily removed for cleaning. It's fairly effective at resisting water, so this is a great solution for a wooden cabinet floor under the sink.

- Or use plastic rug runners—also durable and easy to clean.

Pests in the Cupboard

If you have a problem with weevils or ants, seal up and discard any infested food. Wash and dry the cabinet shelves. To prevent further contamination without chemicals, try one of the following: Leave a few bay leaves or cloves, a thin line of cayenne or black pepper, or a few pieces of mint-flavored gum (wrapped or unwrapped) at the point of infestation.

CABINETS

- *Wooden cabinets, sealed:* Polyurethane cabinets can be wiped clean with a damp cloth or a cloth dipped in an all-purpose cleaning solution, then wiped dry. No waxing or polishing is necessary. If they are dull, use Klean 'N Shine, a product made for this purpose.

- *Wooden cabinets, unsealed:* Clean with a mixture of 10 parts water and 1 part ammonia or Murphy Oil Soap. Either will strip old polish and wax and/or accumulated surface dirt. Then spray on a polish or rub on a wax.

- *Shelves:* See Shelf Solutions, p. 125.
  Also see Laminates.

CAST-IRON SKILLET

- Season by giving it a light coat of oil, then leaving it in a 300-degree oven for 2–3 hours. Put a coffee filter in the pan when you put it away to absorb moisture and prevent rusting. Whenever you use it subsequently, you just need to wipe it out—or use a little soap or water—but the key is to give it a light coat of oil and make sure it's dry.

- *Food sticking, pan rusting, or pan turning food black:* re-season.
- *Crusted-on foods:* Use a pumice stone or rub with a bit of salt.
- *Outside of pan black:* Not a problem, really. But if it bothers you, turn the pan upside down on newspaper, spray it with a commercial oven cleaner, leave it overnight, rinse.

A Single Point of Light

Working in a dark cramped space while you're cleaning the back of a cupboard or dark corner of the closet? Get some light on the subject by attaching a night-light to an extension cord. And paint the walls white, next chance you get.

CERAMIC TILE COUNTERTOPS

- Clean with mild, all-purpose detergent and water.
- Bon Ami or Bar Keepers Friend will remove most stains.
- For stubborn stains, try the following: hydrogen peroxide on blood; hydrogen peroxide or bleach on food and drink; club soda and water on grease.
- To remove ink, keep the surface wet with bleach until the stain disappears, then rinse and dry.

COFFEE BREWER AND COFFEEPOT

- ✿ To clean the brewing portion of a drip-style machine, put in a clean paper filter or cover a permanent filter with paper toweling that you can discard afterward and brew a pot of plain vinegar, followed by a pot of plain water. Save the vinegar for future use: You can run it through the machine four or five times.
- Use a mild all-purpose cleaner on the exterior of the machine, and for stubborn stains use Bon Ami. Put any removable part (such as the piece that holds the filter) in the dishwasher.

COFFEE GRINDER, DIRTY

- Use a pastry brush to clean coffee off the blades. If the blades can't be washed, clean them occasionally by grinding plain grits, cornmeal, or oatmeal.

MY READERS TIP ME OFF: Cleaning Coffeepots

Some of my waitress fans have told me that restaurants clean a glass coffeepot by filling it with ¼ cup table salt and 12 ice cubes. They swish that around, leave it for 30 minutes, pour it out, then rinse the pot with cold water.

COLANDER, STICKY

- Remove gummy pasta leftovers by soaking the colander in a grease-removing detergent. To prevent the problem, coat it with nonstick vegetable spray before you use it or soak it in cold water immediately after use so starch can't harden.

Seal and Soak

If you want to soak something overnight, but the water runs out of your kitchen sink too quickly, put a piece of plastic wrap under the drain stopper and you'll have a tight seal.

COOKTOPS AND RANGE TOPS

- *Ceran:* Wipe sugary spills immediately. Use manufacturer-recommended product for routine cleaning. For a stain, make a paste of baking soda and water, spread it on cool stove, leave briefly, then scrape with a plastic scraper or safety razor, keeping surface wet. If you run up against a stubborn stain, use Bon Ami.
- *Glass, smooth:* For routine cleanup use mild detergent or baking soda. Occasionally use special cleaners that protect the surface. (Get them from your dealer.) Dark marks from metal rubbing against the cooktop must be cleaned before heating or they'll remain in the surface permanently. If the mark is from copper, use Bar Keeper Friend. If it's from aluminum, first mix 1 part bleach and 4 parts water, saturate a cloth, and leave it on the mark about an hour. Then use Bar Keepers Friend. Finally, recoat with cleaner/conditioners, wiping off excess and wiping surface dry before use.
- *Glass, black:* Wipe away sugar stains immediately to avoid pitting. Use mild detergent for routine cleanup and rinse thoroughly. If vinegar and water alone don't remove a stain, leave a vinegar-soaked paper towel or cloth in place for 15 minutes, then use a plastic scraper. Don't use abrasives and don't get vinegar on the metal parts. After cleaning, rinse and dry.

    See also Porcelain Enamel, p. 145.

Enough

∧

Right On

If you notice a boilover in the oven when you're removing a dish, take a spray bottle and squirt water on it. Let it set until the oven cools. Use a plastic scraper or a single-edge razor blade to remove stubborn residue.

COPPER POTS

- ⚙ *Lime buildup in copper kettle:* Fill kettle with half hot water and half vinegar and let it stand for a few hours. Or use the commercial product meant for cleaning glass coffeepots. Once lime has dissolved, wash the kettle with soap and water.
- *Lacquered copper:* These are decorative only. Clean with a damp cloth only. Anything else may remove the finish.
- *Tarnished pan, or burn on copper-bottom pot:* Use Bar Keepers Friend.
- Or use the old-fashioned remedy of sprinkling salt on a half a lemon and rubbing the pot, then rinse and wash with hot soapy water and dry as usual.
- Or if you find commercial copper cleaner you like, use it. (And let me know about it. I've never found one I love.)

CORIAN AND OTHER SOLID SURFACE SYNTHETICS

- *General cleanup:* All-purpose cleaner.
- *Cuts and scratches:* Sand scratched surface with 400 grit sandpaper for semigloss/high gloss finishes, 180 or 220 grit on matte/satin.
- *Stains:* Use 1 part bleach to 4 parts water. Spray on, let set till the stain is gone, which should be within a couple of minutes), then rinse off. If that doesn't work out, use Bon Ami or Bar Keepers Friend with a sponge or cloth.

CORK COASTERS, TRIVETS, OR MATS

- Dip in cold water, rub with a smooth pumice stone, rinse in cold water, dry thoroughly. Store in a cool, dry place.

CORK FLOOR, DULL

- Cork with a resistant finish is popular these days. It can be cleaned with a barely damp mop, but check with your manufacturer for any special instructions.
- If it has an acrylic or urethane finish and looks dull, it may need a new coat of clear floor urethane.
- If it has a wax finish, it should be cared for like a hardwood floor. See Wood Floors, pp. 193–197.

COUNTERTOPS

- See Butcher Block, Ceramic Tile, Corian and Other Solid Surface Synthetics, Granite, Laminate Countertops, Stainless Steel. For Marble, see pp. 75–77.

CRISPER DRAWERS

- Use all-purpose cleaner, but if you discover a couple of furry zucchini or black-spotted tomatoes, discard them and wash the crisper with 1 part bleach to 4 parts water to kill any traces of mold.

Liner Notes

Produce gets moldy when too much moisture collects in the crisper drawer. That's why it's a good idea to line the drawer with foam mats sold for this purpose. Make sure it is dry when you return it to the drawer.

Towel Rack

Get a couple of magnetic hooks, stick them on the fridge, and place a curtain rod between them. Presto: a handy place to hang the dish towel.

DISH DRAINBOARD

- ⚙ Stick it in the dishwasher to clean it.
- ⚙ If you see black spots, a sign of mildew, soak it in a solution of ½ cup of bleach to a gallon of water, with a few drops of liquid dishwashing detergent. Rinse after half an hour.
- ⚙ To remove a hard-water stain, tilt the low end of the board so it's flat and pour white vinegar on top, then let it stand overnight. Sponge clean in the morning. Then polish with spray wax and let it dry overnight.

DISHWASHER

- ⚙ Fill the detergent cup in the empty machine with vinegar and run the machine on rinse for a few minutes without any dishes inside; then let it stand a few minutes more; finally let the rinse cycle complete. Use heated (not energy saver) drying.
- If the dishes aren't coming out clean, and you think the ports where the water comes in may be clogged, use a pipe cleaner. In some dishwashers, there is a filter screen (strainer) that can be scrubbed with a stiff brush. Always look for any food particles, pieces of broken glass, or anything else trapped on the screen that might be preventing the water from circulating.
- If there's an odor from dishes that haven't been washed right away, sprinkle ¼ cup of baking soda on the bottom of the dishwasher. In case of a persistent odor, have your disposal unit checked. There's probably food trapped somewhere.
- Food that's collected around the door seal can be wiped away with a cloth and Bon Ami.

DON'TS for the Dishwasher

- Don't use it to wash any of the following:

    Fine crystal: May break.

    Gold-rimmed dishes or glasses, hand-painted china: Designs may come off.

    Antique dinnerware: May crack due to heat.

    Lacquered metal: May peel.

    Gold-plated flatware: Plating may come off.

    Bone-, ivory-, or wood-handled flatware; all wooden ware: May crack.

    Knives: Wooden handles may get dry and split. They also say that knives get dull in the dishwasher, but I've never had that problem.

    Silverware and stainless, together: If they touch in the dishwasher, silver may spot.

DO'S for the Dishwasher

- Put the dishes in the dishwasher so they face the water spray.
- Load like things in the same area—glasses near glasses, dinner plates near dinner plates, spoons and forks in one compartment, knives and soup spoons in another—and you'll be able to unload faster.
- Loop a wide elastic band over small items so they stay in place, or put an oven rack over top rack.

Dirty or Clean?

I couldn't always tell whether the dishwasher had done its thing until I discovered this trick. Leave an uncapped spice or other small bottle upright in a front corner of the top rack. When dishes are clean, it will be full of water. Empty the bottle when you unload and return it right side up.

The Right Way to Wash Dishes by Hand

Always scrape, rinse, and stack the dishes before you tackle the actual washing. That will help you get organized and prevent food from caking on.

(continued)

Start with the least greasy items and move to the greasiest—so begin with the glassware, then move on to cutlery, plates, and pots. Place each item into hot soapy water, then rinse in clean water. If you don't have a two-section sink, fill a dishpan with the soapy water and use the one-section sink for rinsing. (As I said before, no towel-drying. If you must dry it quickly, set a fan nearby.)

Quick Setting

When you empty the dishwasher after dinner, wrap a flatware place setting in a napkin for each family member. Children are able to help set the table, and the job gets done faster.

Breaking Point

Line the sink with a towel when you're washing fine glassware. And slide the glasses in the water edgewise. If you put them in bottom first, sudden expansion from the heat may cause them to crack.

DRAIN, CLOGGED

- If you haven't acted preventively (see Drain Solution, p. 120), you may have a problem.
- If you suspect that grease is forming the clog, point a hair dryer set at medium about 6–8 inches from the pipe and move it gently back and forth for a few minutes. Then run hot water through the drain.
- A narrow brush designed for poking down the drain can sometimes remove clogged debris.
- If the drain is still sluggish, pour in a cup of baking soda, followed by a kettle of boiling water. If that doesn't do the job, dissolve 2 tablespoons of washing soda in a quart of hot water and pour it slowly down the drain.
- Or run a garden hose into the house, push the nozzle into the drain as far as possible, wrap a towel around the hose to close the drain opening fully, and hold on

while someone else turns on the outdoor faucet. Whatever is clogged should be forced out by water pressure.

- If all else fails, try a commercial drain cleaner. See box below.
- And if that fails, call in a pro. CAUTION: Stay away from that drain until the pro has handled the situation.

Cautions for Drain Cleaners

These chemicals are products of the last resort that will eventually harm your pipes and must be used with the greatest care. When you add water, the chemicals in drain cleaners cause it to boil in your pipes; the heat that's created melts the clog and starts an agitating action of little bits of metal that also promote cleanup.

- Don't use a plunger after an unsuccessful treatment with a drain cleaner, because the caustic product can be splashed up at you. Call in a pro.
- Don't put your face near a drain after you've used a drain cleaner since acid may cause water in the pipe to boil up.
- If the label says that a cleaner is not for fully clogged drains, believe it. You need a pro or a mechanical device to open up the clog.
- Don't use drain cleaner in a backed-up toilet. If there's leftover toilet-cleaning product in the bowl, adding drain cleaner may create a toxic gas.
- NEVER MIX DRAIN CLEANER WITH ANY OTHER PRODUCT, including ammonia, bleach, or another drain cleaner. Results can create toxic and possibly fatal gases.

DRIP PANS AND REFLECTOR BOWLS

- Refer to 21 Ways to Save Kitchen Cleanup Time, p. 116, to avoid cleaning these in the future.
- ✪ Put them in the dishwasher if they're soiled.
- ✪ Or pour some ammonia in a plastic bag, slip them in, and leave it sealed overnight. Turn your face away when you open the bag since the fumes will be pretty

strong. The best place to do this is outside, so you can just hose down the pans.

- Or put down a towel, place newspaper on top, give them a shot of oven spray, leave them a while, then rinse.
- Blue, gold, or brown stains on chrome bowls can't be removed: They're probably caused by overheating. This happens when you use pans that are larger than the cooking unit or that don't have a flat bottom (such as woks and teakettles, or pans that are damaged). Being discolored doesn't make them any less functional.

ELECTRICAL APPLIANCES

- Exterior surfaces of all small electrical appliances (blenders, can openers, etc.) can be wiped with all-purpose cleaner.
- If appliances can be taken apart, put nonelectrical pieces in the dishwasher.

Can Do

To keep the water from draining out while you're soaking the bowl of a food processor, use a film canister as a plug—it's just the right size.

ENAMEL COOKWARE

- If the lasagna or other food is stuck to the pan, sprinkle some baking soda or automatic dishwashing detergent and water on the spot and leave it overnight. Or combine 1 quart of water with 3 tablespoons baking soda, boil 15 minutes, and let the mixture stand to cool. Then use a plastic scrubbing pad to rub the spot away.

FIXTURE, CEILING, DIRTY
- ✿ Most glass fixtures can safely be put into the dishwasher. Check with the manufacturer if you're not sure.

FLOORS
See Laminate Floors, Linoleum, Terrazzo in this section. See also Wood Floors, pp. 193–197, and Marble, pp. 75–77.

Cutting the Ice
Have a freezer that requires defrosting? After you've done the job, give the interior a coating of cooking oil or vegetable spray. Ice will build up slower and release more quickly.

Cold Storage
Where to stow all the freezer food while you're defrosting?
- Use a large cooler.
- The washing machine is another good spot. It's roomy, it's insulated, and any moisture that drips off won't be a problem. But cover the shaft with a towel first so the cold doesn't make it brittle.
- Your electric oven is another good spot—it's insulated too. (The heat from the pilot light in a gas oven makes it unacceptable for this purpose.)

FREEZER
- For cleaning and odor problems, see Refrigerator, p. 147.
- It's time to defrost when the ice is ½ inch thick. (The longer you let it go, the harder it is to do.) Turn off the motor and all controls and empty everything out. (See Cold Storage above.) Some impatient types prefer to wave a hair dryer at it, or fill the freezer with bowls of hot water, but the easiest, least messy way is to let the ice melt naturally. You shouldn't chip away with a tool, because you might damage the unit, but you can scrape away slush and water with a plastic dustpan or

a squeegee onto a plastic tray, and dump it out in the sink.

- If you're defrosting a chest-style freezer, pick up the liquid with a sponge mop and use a dustpan to scrape away and pick up ice quickly and easily.
- When defrosting is complete, wipe away the condensation, sponge-clean the freezer walls with soapy water, then dry thoroughly. Plug everything back in and turn the controls on, and wait ½ hour before replacing food. Wait until controls reach 0 degrees before adding anything new. (Maximum temperature should be 5 degrees.)

Marking Time

Does everyone have what may be mastodon meat in the back of the freezer, or is it only me? It's helpful to mark everything with a USE BY date (rather than the date you store it), to prompt you to cook up some of these souvenirs and discard whatever's too far gone.

GARBAGE CAN

- To prevent odor in an outdoor pail, leave a couple of inches of cat box filler in the bottom and change it occasionally.
- Keep animal pests away by spraying the can with ammonia or with garlic or cayenne pepper spray from the garden shop. Take care when you use the cayenne not to transfer any from your hands to your eyes: It burns. Or try one of the new deer repellent products that don't need to be reapplied after rain.

GARBAGE DISPOSAL

- To clean, pour white vinegar into an ice cube tray reserved for this purpose, make cubes, and drop them in one at a time while running the disposal. Six should do the job.

- Or use plain cubes, pour in ½ cup of baking soda, and when the mixture is mush, turn on the cold water to flush it out.
- Or use a toilet bowl brush reserved for this purpose. Dip it in dishwashing liquid and scrub.

MY VIEWERS TIP ME OFF: Cleaning the Disposal
If you're a recycler, you'll love this use for leftover citrus rinds sent by a fan from Florida. Save them in the freezer and occasionally toss a few down the garbage disposal to prevent odor.

And the Band Stays On
- Get a 1-inch-wide piece of elastic slightly shorter than the diameter of your garbage pail and sew the ends together. Slip this over the plastic bag that you use to line the pail so it won't ever slip down.
- Or use 2 jumbo spring-action binder clips to hold it on.

GLASS COOKWARE
- Use a cloth or plastic scrubber sprinkled with Bon Ami.
- *To remove scorches:* Sprinkle with baking soda or automatic dishwasher detergent, leave overnight, rinse, and wash as usual. Or put the bakeware on newspaper, spray it with oven cleaner, leave it a few minutes, then rinse and wash as usual.

GLASSWARE, CLOUDY OR FILMY
- Rub it with vinegar. If the film disappears, try one or more of the following. (1) Clean the dishwasher by putting it through a cycle without dishes, filling the cup with citric acid (from the drugstore) instead of soap and setting it to heated drying. (2) Make sure detergent is fresh, not lumpy. (3) Use a rinsing agent such as Jet-

Dry. (4) Cut the amount of detergent you use by half if you have soft water or use softener if water is very hard.

- If the film remains, the glassware is permanently etched. (A clue: In the earliest stages of etching, the glassware looks iridescent.) There's nothing you can do about this. So buy inexpensive glassware and replace it periodically.

Hot and Cold

If one glass is stuck inside another, forcing them apart may cause a breakage and you'll probably cut your hand. Instead, fill the top glass with cold water and dip the lower one in hot water; they'll come apart with no problem. (The same trick works with stuck-together pots.)

GOLD-PLATED FLATWARE
- If it needs polishing, coat with a paste of baking soda, rinse, and buff dry.

GRANITE
- *For routine cleaning:* mild dishwashing liquid or stone soap from a hardware store or stone dealer. For polished granite, use a stone polish product from the hardware store or stone dealer.
- See also Tabletops, p. 185.

LAMINATE COUNTERTOPS
- These are easily stained, so I always use a cutting board when working with any potentially staining item—from blueberries to Kool-Aid.
- Use a mild, all-purpose cleaner for routine cleaning. Manufacturers advise against the use of any cleaner containing acid, alkali, or chlorine. Countertop cleaners contain these ingredients, as do drain cleaners,

bleach, rust removers, and lime scale removers, so always read labels.

- For miscellaneous stains, use Bar Keepers Friend or Bon Ami.
- Certain stains may be permanent—among them, hair dye, bluing, Mercurochrome, and peroxide. You may be able to tone them down by dabbing on a paste of baking soda and water to "pull out" the stain. Don't rub it; just leave it for about 15 minutes, then wipe with a clean nonabrasive cloth. If it seems to be working, repeat.
- *A last resort only for ink stains:* Try equal parts bleach and water left on the spot for only a minute or two. Since manufacturers recommend against the use of bleach, do this at your own risk and try it first in an inconspicuous spot. Remember never to mix bleach with acids, alkalis, or ammonias since toxic gases will result.
- *Dull:* I wouldn't bother, but if you want a shine, choose a commercial polish.
- *Heat damage:* If you've had a blister followed by a crater, use Seamfill (sold at Formica dealers), white wood filler, or white sandless grout. Sand lightly and cover with wax to match the shine of the rest of the counter. If the laminate is colored, you can paint the area in the closest color you can find, and then wax.

LAMINATE FLOORS
- Damp-mop with plain water.
- In case of heavy soiling, use ½ cup ammonia to a gallon of water. No soap; it will cause dulling.

LIGHT SWITCH, GRIMY
- Spray on all-purpose cleaner, let it sit, and scrub with an old toothbrush.

Shard Labor

When a glass item breaks in the kitchen, the best tool to pick up small slivers is a cordless vac. In a pinch, use a piece of soft bread. You won't cut your fingers as you might through paper.

LINOLEUM

- *Routine cleaning:* Damp-mop with all-purpose cleaner.
- *Visible grime:* Use either water-based or solvent-based wax. Don't use ammonia or strong alkalis on linoleum because they may eventually cause it to crack.
- *Dingy and gray:* If you've been using a water-based wax, get a stripper/cleaner made for linoleum, follow the directions on the can, then rewax. Or check with manufacturer.
- *Scuffed:* Rub gently with baking soda on a damp sponge. Or check with the manufacturer.
- *Yellowing:* May be age, but also may be wax. Sometimes so-called nonyellowing wax does turn yellow either because you put down too much or you laid a second coat before the first was completely dry. Use a liquid wax stripper/cleaner, following the directions on the can. Or rent a floor scrubber/polisher to scrub on a stripping product and then to wax and buff the floor.

MICROWAVE OVEN

- *Cooked-on food:* Put a damp dishcloth or paper towel on top of the stain, turn the oven to high, and microwave for 15 seconds. Or boil a cup of water in a 2-cup glass measure in the oven for several minutes. Either way, moisture will condense on the interior and dried food will be softened so it can be wiped up.
- *Odor:* Add 2 tablespoons of lemon juice or baking soda to a cup of water and let it boil about 5 minutes, then let it stand about 10 minutes. Wipe.

- *Door streaked and dirty:* Use glass cleaner and a single-edge razor (be sure to keep surface wet) or plastic credit card to scrape it if necessary.
- *Door scratched by steel wool pad:* Use plastic polish or nongel toothpaste, rubbed on gently.

NONSTICK PAN, STICKY

- An invisible film of grease or food may be causing the problem. Boil 2 tablespoons of baking soda, ½ cup vinegar, and a cup of water in the pan for a few minutes. Then use all-purpose cleaner and a plastic scrubber. Wash it well with hot water and all-purpose cleaner.

News for Noses

Odors will disappear from plastic containers and thermoses overnight if you pack them with crumpled newspaper and put the lid on tightly.

OVEN, CONTINUOUS CLEAN

- Remove stubborn spots with a plastic scraper or razor and rinse with water.
- To catch spills, line the oven floor with a length of heavy-duty aluminum foil. When the bake element is cool, lift it just enough to get the feet off the oven floor and slide in the foil, keeping it unwrinkled. When you lower the bake element, make sure all the feet are flat.
- Never use a commercial oven cleaner or any product not recommended by the manufacturer.

OVEN, CONVENTIONAL, DIRTY

- See Ammonia, p. 43, and Oven Cleaner, p. 45.
- Or sprinkle the bottom of the oven with automatic dishwasher detergent, cover with wet paper towels, and let stand for a few hours.

OVEN, SELF-CLEANING

- Follow the manufacturer's instructions. Clean the gasket with a heavy-duty cleanser before you turn on the oven, or food will bake on. (Your manual will explain how to remove it.) Use white vinegar to clean any dirt that remains. Do not use any commercial cleaners. The oven may heat any residue and create toxic fumes.
- If you want better access to the inside of the oven so you can clean it more easily, check your manual to see if it's possible to remove the oven door.
- Do not clean or bend the fiberglass seal.
- Clean the outside with mild abrasive and water.

OVEN DOORS, GLASS

- Spray on a glass cleaner, and use a scraping tool to remove any burned-on food. (Make sure the surface is wet to prevent scratching.)

OVEN RACKS, BLACKENED

- Put racks in a plastic garbage bag, pour in a couple of cups of ammonia, seal the bag with a twist-tie, and leave it outdoors for 24 hours. Be sure to point the bag away from you when you open it, then rinse everything off with the garden hose. (Do not use this process on aluminum.)
- Or soak them in your tub on top of a towel. Draw enough hot water to cover and add a cup of degreasing all-purpose cleaner; or sprinkle a cup of automatic dishwashing detergent over all and let them soak clean.
- Or put them in the dishwasher. Stop the machine before the dry cycle and take them out. Since the dirt will be loosened, it will be easy to clean off with Bon Ami or, if need be, a stronger scouring agent.

MY READERS TIP ME OFF: Cleaning Ovens
An appliance repairman tells me he quick-cleans a conventional oven by warming it to 150 degrees, turning it off, then spraying the interior with Fantastik. (I think any degreasing all-purpose cleaner would work as well.) In 15 minutes or less, the grease will rub off easily.

Bright Idea
Put a paper cup over the oven bulb when you're cleaning a standard oven. The cup will protect it from your spray cleaner and still keep the oven illuminated as you work.

PLASTIC STORAGE CONTAINERS, STAINED
- ⚙ Just put them in the sun.

DON'TS for Porcelain Enamel
- Don't use bleach full-strength. It removes many stains, but if used full-strength it may damage the finish.
- Don't leave vinegar, lemons, or any acid-containing cleaners in the sink for long periods. They may stain it.
- Don't use abrasive products or scrub excessively. If the finish is worn away, porcelain will become more susceptible to staining.
- Don't let cleaning products stand on the surface. Always rinse, then dry the enamel after you clean it.

PORCELAIN ENAMEL
- Bar Keepers Friend will remove most stains.
- *Burnt-on food:* Dip a damp cloth in mild all-purpose cleaner and drop it on the spot, or pour a couple of

drops of boiling water on it. In a minute or two, it will soften up and you can use a nylon scrubber or scraping tool to rub it off.

- *Coffee:* Rub with a damp cloth dipped in baking soda or other nonabrasive cleansers.
- *Grease:* Scrub with Simple Green. If it's very dirty try ½ cup trisodium phosphate and 1 gallon hot water. Follow cautions on package.
- *Hard water:* Mix equal parts vinegar and water, apply with a plastic scrubber. Afterward, rinse and dry. Or try Bar Keeper Friend.
- *Mildew:* May occur if a layer of greasy film has accumulated. Wipe with 1 part bleach and 4 parts water in a ventilated area. Rinse.
- *Plastic melted onto:* If a plastic bag or container has melted onto a porcelain enamel stove, hold a hair dryer set to medium 6–8 inches away and wave it back and forth. As the heat causes the plastic to soften, scrape it away with a credit card or (being very careful not to scratch) with a putty knife.
- *Rust stains:* Use Bar Keeper Friend.
- *Soap scum:* Rub with baking soda and water, Bon Ami, or Bar Keeper Friend.

POTS AND PANS
See also Aluminum Cookware, Copper Pots, Enamel Cookware, Glass Cookware, Stainless Steel.

- *Inside stained black:* Spray the area with oven cleaner, let set a few minutes, then wash. (Not for aluminum pans.)
- *Bottoms blackened:* There is really no reason to clean the bottoms of pots. But if you like them to shine, here's the easiest way. Set the pot on newspaper, spray with oven cleaner, let sit briefly, and then rinse. Repeat if necessary.

Get Rattled

You won't burn the bottom of your steamer or double boiler if you place a jar, lid, or marbles in the bottom section. When you hear the rattling, you'll know the water has boiled away.

Don't Let Your Cookware Go to Pot

- Keep the gas flame low on metal pots, not crawling up the side. You'll have fewer carbon deposits to clean and less chance of permanent blue/green heat discolorations.
- There are heat diffusers you can buy to place between your pot and the flame and to keep pots simmering. They also reduce the chance of heat damage to your pot. Or just stack one grate on top of another and that does the job just fine. Or make a "rope" of aluminum foil that you thread under and over the grate and set the pot on top of it.
- Don't take pots off the heat and plunge them into cold water. Sudden temperature changes cause warping.
- Don't store salty or very acidic foods in pots and don't soak them in chlorine bleach. Both cause pitting.

PYREX DISHES
- See Glass Cookware, p. 139.

REFRIGERATOR
- Check your manual for cleaning suggestions.
- *Food stains inside:* If an all-purpose cleaner fails to remove food stains, use Bon Ami or Bar Keepers Friend and a wet sponge or nylon scrubber. See also Crisper Drawers, p. 131.
- *Odor:* Make sure there's not an old piece of Gorgonzola cheese or a rotting onion behind or beside the fridge. Then check the refrigerator drip pan. If you don't know how to find it and have never cleaned it, it may be the source of your problem. Check your manual, call the

Enough
^

manufacturer, or check the manufacturer's Web page if you need help locating and removing it. Wash it with baking soda and water or let it soak for a while. If an odor persists, spoiled food may have dripped onto insulation and you need to call for service.

- *Power outage:* Throw away all the spoiled food, fill the shelves with crumpled newspaper or large shallow pans spread with ground coffee or activated charcoal, shut the door, and don't open it for 2–3 days. Repeat if necessary. When we had a serious power outage one summer, I was out of town for a couple of weeks. I didn't dare open my freezer, which was stored in the garage. Fortunately, the temperature dropped below freezing and the food refroze, so I could remove it, odor-free. This is one compensation for living in Minneapolis.

- *Rubber gaskets around door:* Remove stains with a mild solution of bleach and water, vinegar and water, or baking soda on a damp cloth, rubbing alcohol, or whitewall tire cleaner.

Scents and No Scents

- A cotton ball saturated with vanilla extract leaves a pleasant odor in the fridge.
- An open can of coffee grounds or box of baking soda deodorizes the refrigerator.
- I also like the volcanic rock that comes in a net bag and can be placed in the sun to reactivate its odor-absorbing properties; available in many stores.

Makeover Magic

If an appliance works well but is scratched or the wrong color, have it repainted. Look up Appliances—Painting and Refinishing or Auto Body Paint Shops in the Yellow Pages. With a new finish, it will be easy to clean, and there's a wide range of color choices. Note: Cooking surfaces get too hot to be repainted.

RUST, ON METAL

- Sprinkle Bar Keepers Friend on a cork or potato, then rub it on the stain.

SILVER, TARNISHED

- See Silver Cloth/Silver Polish, p. 47.
- If you don't have any silver cleaner on hand, you can improvise with a paste of 3 parts baking soda to 1 part water. Apply with a damp sponge or soft cloth, rinse, and buff.
- ❂ The fastest method of cleaning is "electrolytic" polishing. In a nonaluminum pan, put a small square of aluminum foil, water, a tablespoon of salt, and 2 tablespoons of baking soda for each quart of water. Bring to a boil. Add silver, submerging it completely, boil 2–3 minutes (or until the tarnish is gone). Remove silver with tongs, wash in hot sudsy water, rinse, and dry. CAUTION: This method removes all oxidation, so shading is lost; fine silver may look like plate. It is also not recommended for "antiqued" silver, silver plate, or pieces with hollow handles fastened with cement (such as silver-handled wooden salad serving pieces or carving knives with stainless blades).

DO'S for Sterling Silver

- Use the specially treated cloth bags for storage (sold in the silver department of department stores and in jewelry and hardware stores) or line the drawer with the treated cloth (available from fabric stores).
- To prevent tarnish, push all air out of the silver storage bag before you close it.
- A piece of camphor in the storage bag or cabinet draws moisture from the silver. But camphor shouldn't touch the silver.

(continued)

Enough
∧

- Store silver away from dampness and direct light. A single light-bulb shining on silver will cause it to tarnish faster than if it's in a dark, dry place.
- Use it every day and tarnish won't accumulate.

DON'TS for Sterling Silver

- Don't wear rubber gloves when you polish (they create tarnish) and don't use rubber bands on silver (they may create stains).
- Never wrap silver in plastic wrap. It may trap moisture that leaves spots.
- Never put stainless steel flatware and silverware in the same basket. Direct contact may cause spotting on silver that cannot be removed.
- Don't put knives in the dishwasher: The high heat can affect the cement that holds the stainless blade to the sterling handle.
- Soaking overnight or for a long time can damage sterling.
- Don't store silver when wet. It may develop pits or dark spots that won't disappear without a lot of buffing.

STAINLESS STEEL

- "Stainless" steel can actually stain and may rust or pit. It may be harmed by chlorine bleach (or cleansers that contain it), muriatic acid, and certain chemical additives in liquid soaps. See Don'ts for Stainless Steel, p. 151.
- For routine cleaning, use all-purpose cleaner or alcohol. Or apply baking soda on a damp sponge.
- *Cookware:* When soap and water don't do the job, sprinkle on Bon Ami and use a plastic scrubber, or use the edge of a credit card to remove burned-on food. Stains that come from cooking dried fruit containing sulfur dioxide or food with a high starch content can be removed with a stainless steel–cleaning product. But those blue/gold stains are permanent, a result of

overheating. See Don't Let Your Cookware Go to Pot, p. 147.

- *Sinks and countertops:* The secret to keeping them looking good is simple: Wipe them dry after use. But some stainless steel sinks have a nickel plating on them, which makes them very shiny. If this surface is worn off, you may not be able to get the sink shiny again. Use Bar Keepers Friend for rust stains, rubbing alcohol for spots, and oven cleaner (sprayed on for 15 minutes, then rinsed) for the most stubborn stains.

DON'TS for Stainless Steel

- Don't let cleaning products stand in the sink or on a countertop (especially chlorine or solvents). Rinse after use and wipe dry so chemicals don't stain and mineral deposits don't build up.
- Don't leave sponges or cleaning pads on a stainless sink or countertop.
- Don't leave any rubber mats on stainless steel. Otherwise solutions may get "trapped" below it and eventually cause staining.
- Do not use any abrasives on a stainless steel pot or surface without checking the care instructions from the manufacturer.
- Don't use steel wool on a stainless sink since bits may lodge in the sink and get rusty.
- Do not rub against the grain.

MY VIEWERS TIP ME OFF: Cleaning Stainless Steel

A woman with a badly stained stainless steel sink took drastic measures. She opened the windows for ventilation, poured boiling water on her sink to coat it, sprayed on ammonia, then covered the area with a leaf bag taped in place. "I left the house for 24 hours, then rinsed the area when I returned," she told me. Result: "Neighbors thought I'd had a new sink installed."

STOVE

- See also Burner Pans, Cooktops and Range Tops, Porcelain Enamel, Stainless Steel.
- *Greasy knobs and burner pans:* Pull off knobs, remove drip pans, and let them soak in 1 gallon of water and ¼ cup of dishwasher detergent. Rinse clean.
- *Gummy boilover:* If you have an extremely gooey mess that can't be budged, spray the area with WD-40, then clean up with all-purpose cleaning spray.

TEAKETTLES

- ✿ *Corning glass, stained:* Boil 2 parts vinegar to 1 part water for 15 minutes.
- ✿ *Metal, water-stained:* To remove white deposits, pour half vinegar, half water into the pot, then bring it to a boil and lower heat to a simmer for 15 minutes. Repeat if necessary.

TERRAZZO

- Since this type of floor is a mixture of marble and other substances, like marble it needs to be cleaned with some caution. Don't use vinegar or any other acid-based cleaner, alkalis, or other harsh cleaners. Use an all-purpose neutral cleaner and leave it on the floor long enough for grime-dissolving action to take place but not long enough for it to dry out, as dirt will be reabsorbed. Cover it with an acrylic floor product, not wax (which is slippery).

TOASTER OR TOASTER OVEN

- Use an all-purpose mild cleaner on the exterior of a plastic appliance and on the chrome. Empty the crumb tray from time to time. If you have crumbs stuck inside, unplug the toaster and use a pipe cleaner or a thin brush called a percolator brush.

- *Dull chrome:* If it desperately needs shining, polish with dry—never damp—superfine steel wool (grade 0000).
- *Glass window dirty:* Spray on all-purpose cleaner. Let it set. Scrape with single-edge razor, keeping surface wet as you work to avoid scratches.
- *Plastic melted onto:* If a plastic bag or plastic wrap has melted on the outside of a toaster, reheat the toaster until it is warm, then unplug it. Then use a plastic credit card or single-edge razor to scrape, keeping area wet to avoid scratches.

TRASH COMPACTOR

- *Odor:* Air freshener or charcoal filter may need replacing.
- *Soiled:* Turn off the compactor, remove the key knob (if there is one), and clean all the parts—drawer if it lifts out, bin, bag caddy—with warm, soapy water. If the rim that presses on the garbage is particularly greasy, add some ammonia to the soapy water. Rinse thoroughly, dry, replace drawer, and install a new bag or reusable bin.

Tile Trick

- If a vinyl floor tile comes loose or develops a bulge, put a piece of aluminum foil over the tile and run a hot iron across the top a few times to soften the glue. Then put a couple of heavy books on the tile to flatten it.
- The same method, minus the heavy books, can be used to remove floor tile.

VINYL FLOORING

- For routine cleaning, use a small amount of all-purpose cleaner and you won't need to rinse. (The more cleaner, the more foam you create.)
- *Dingy:* May be caused by insufficient rinsing or residue from a cleaning product. Use a self-polishing cleaner and water, and repeat if needed.
- *Dull:* "No wax" flooring doesn't mean "no maintenance." It eventually needs a gloss-renewing product sold especially for this purpose. Or use a water-based, self-cleaning, no-wax floor care product, ideally only three or four times a year. Eventually that builds up, too, and leaves a dull film. Buy a stripper cleaner, or use ½ cup vinegar and ½ gallon water. Apply the solution, allow 3 minutes for the product to soften, and wipe with a clean, damp mop. Then rewax. You may eventually need to wax about every year or so and strip after every two or three waxings.
- *Grease:* Add a few drops of vinegar to the cleaning solution.
- *Kool-Aid stain:* Mix half vinegar and half water, apply, and leave for several minutes. Then wet with 3% hydrogen peroxide solution. Neutralize this with a vinegar rinse (¼ cup to a gallon of water), then rinse again with plain water. Or try liquid abrasive cleaner, but only as a last resort.
- *Scratches or burns:* The good enough housekeeper might not want to attempt this, especially since results won't be perfect. But if you're game, find a touchup paint of the right color and apply carefully with a fine-hair brush. Work carefully—it's hard to remove. Or sand the burn mark with fine sandpaper, rinse with a solution of 1 cup vinegar in a quart of water, then apply acrylic paint mixed to match with a small brush. After 15–20 minutes, seal with acrylic varnish. A buffable water-based wax containing silicone may fill in

scratches too. Apply sparingly from damp mop head or with a machine, then buff. Repeat in high-traffic areas.

- *Scuffed:* Use Bon Ami or baking soda on a damp sponge. Stronger products may scratch vinyl. Then use WD-40 if there is residue. Clean that with mild detergent and water or you'll have a skating rink.

- *Sticky:* May be due to insufficient rinsing when you applied polish or as a result of applying a second coat of polish before the first had dried completely. Mix ¼ cup Murphy Oil Soap in a gallon of water. Apply with sponge mop, then rinse the area with warm water.

- *Yellowing:* Sometimes the area under a floor mat or rug just turns color and the yellow cannot be removed. Or so-called nonyellowing wax does turn yellow. The cause may be too much wax, laying a second coat before the first was dry, or dirt caught between coats of wax. Use stripper/cleaner for no-wax floors, following label instructions, or try the home remedy below.

Homemade Stripper for No-Wax Vinyl

Mix ½ cup ammonia, 1 cup laundry detergent, and 1 gallon of warm water. Put on a test area, which should turn cloudy and soft in a couple of minutes. Otherwise, add up to another ½ cup of ammonia. Use either water- or solvent-based wax afterward.

Pros and Cons of Waxes

On vinyl, you can use either a water- or solvent-based wax.

- Water-based wax is self-polishing, but over time it builds up and has to be stripped.
- Solvent-based wax needs buffing but doesn't build up. A new application cleans away the old one.

WAFFLE IRON

- Newer models are mostly "nonstick," but if the iron needs seasoning, brush on corn or other oil, heat it, then bake a waffle, which will absorb the extra fat. Throw that waffle away, then use the iron. Afterward, don't wash with soap; just brush or wipe dry with paper towel. If waffles begin to stick, wash the iron with soap and water, dry it, and reseason.

WALLS, PAINTED

- The problem with cleaning grease or other stains off the kitchen wall is that once you start, you often have to do the whole darned wall.
- Start with the gentlest remedy on latex painted walls. Use a paste of baking soda and water left on for an hour, then sponged off. Or dissolve old-fashioned dry laundry starch in water. Dip a brush into this solution and "paint" it on the walls. When it's dry, rub it with a soft brush or a clean cloth. This removes stains without harming the paint.
- On semigloss or gloss finishes, you can try something stronger. Use an all-purpose degreasing product. If that doesn't work, dissolve ¼ cup of trisodium phosphate in 1 gallon of warm water, put on rubber gloves, and dip a cloth or sponge in the solution. If grease spots remain, cover them with clear shellac to prevent the oil from bleeding through, then paint with a fresh color.
- See Wall Shield, p. 157.

Wall Shield

- Keep a spray bottle filled with water or a dilute ammonia/water solution to mist over grease spatters and wipe them right away. They're much easier to clean when they're fresh than after they've dried.
- For protection, since a painted wall or wallpaper backsplash area behind the stove is always a target for flying grease, have a piece of Plexiglas cut to size at a hardware store or home center and screw it into place. It's easy to wipe clean.
- See also suggestions for cutting down splatter in 21 Ways to Save Kitchen Cleanup Time, p. 116.

WOK, RUST SPOTS ON

- Remove rust from a wok that lacks a nonstick finish by using a cork or potato sprinkled with Bon Ami or Bar Keepers Friend. Wash with warm, soapy water, dry, then cover with a thin coat of mineral oil. Repeat after each use to prevent rusting.

WOODEN SALAD BOWL

- If it seems dry, relubricate it with mineral oil, wiped on, then rubbed off.

ELEVEN

The Living Room and Dining Room

> **Good enough housekeeping** is cleaning off the handprint without going on to wash the entire wall.

 *Dejunk*

The living room and dining room often have a lot of decorative "stuff" hanging around for the same reason that the famous mountaineer George Mallory gave when someone asked him why he wanted to climb Mount Everest: "Because it's there." Maybe it shouldn't be. Get rid of clutter and turn it back from the "cleaning" room into the "living" room.

DO'S in a Living Room

- Drapes are a pain to clean, they're dust catchers, and they fade unless they have a really thick and heavy lining, which makes them even more difficult to clean. You're better off with curtains that can be washed or blinds with wide slats, which are easier to clean than narrow ones. Use blackout shades in addition if you want to prevent light from coming in; they're useful to pull during the day to keep upholstery and carpets from fading.

- When you paint, always ask the store to recommend a good quality brand. The difference in price between brands is generally relatively small. If you usually pay pros to do the job, you'll save big-time because better-quality paint lasts longer than cheaper paint and you won't need another paint job as quickly. But don't pay just for a designer brand, thinking that it's better quality. I have found these brands often require extra coats. Most paint stores can custom-blend house brands to match any designer color you like.

- Nylon carpeting is a lot less expensive than wool and much more stain resistant.

- Orientals hide soil and footprints best, but if you're going with a solid color, the most practical style is a combination cut and loop pile that may be described as a twist or a frieze (pronounced *freeze*).

- Yes, of course the dog and the children will soil that light-colored couch. Buy something inexpensive and plan to replace it when everyone's matured and better trained. For other ideas, see box on choosing upholstery, next page.

- If you have upholstered furniture near a window, pull the shades or draw the blinds so color won't fade.

- Put in vinyl, double-insulated windows and save yourself the trouble of dealing with storm windows.

THE GOOD ENOUGH HOUSEKEEPER'S GUIDE TO CHOOSING UPHOLSTERY FABRICS

FABRIC	PROS	CONS
Brocade (usually silk or cotton linen)		Not for hard or continuous wear; gets greasy in heavily used areas
Damask	Wears well; doesn't absorb dust	Easily stained
Velvet (silk, nylon, cotton)		Not for hard, constant wear
Corduroy	Durable	
Textural weaves (raw silk and others)	Durable	Strong textures absorb a lot of dust; can fray
Tapestry (usually part wool)	Durable, hides wear; soil resistant; easy to clean	
Denim	Doesn't get dusty; doesn't stain easily	
Vinyl, plastic	Shampoos easily	

PROBLEM: Too many knickknacks.

 • Pick up every single item—the outdated photos, the wilted or hopelessly dirty artificial flowers, the house gifts you never liked but feel obliged to display—off the coffee table, the end tables, and the TV stand and decide whether it's really worth hanging onto. If you're not quite ready to give or throw any item away, I suggest that as a first step, you put them out of sight. See the Box Trick, p. 21, item 11.

PROBLEM: Too much equipment.

Take a good look at what you've got in the hutch and sideboard to see if it's really appropriate for your needs. If your life in no way resembles anything that's ever appeared on *Masterpiece Theatre*, you will probably never serve soup from a tureen at your table or need an oyster plate. If you're a buffet kind of person, you don't really need the cups and saucers for fifteen. Get rid of anything you are unlikely to use and that you don't really love. Here are some of the things that wound up at my local thrift shop the last time I dejunked my dining room: a set of fish knives and forks, a bowl with a nutcracker in the middle, and a fondue pot. (I know fondue's back in fashion, but I never served it the last time, either.)

Table Space Savers

- Stow the table pad out of sight right below the table. Find the right sizes of hooks or angle irons and install them so pads can rest on top.
- To expand your small table for occasional needs, have a much larger top made of plywood in two or more sections that can be connected with a simple hook and eye. Once you put a tablecloth on top, your guests won't know they're dining on plywood rather than mahogany.

Enough

THE BASIC SUPPLIES FOR GOOD ENOUGH LIVING ROOM
AND DINING ROOM CLEANING

All-purpose cleaner and cloth
Cobweb eliminating spray
Dry sponge
Dusting cloths
Feather duster
Lambswool duster
Ostrich feather duster
Toothbrush
Vacuum cleaner

DAILY
NEATEN UP.

• Clear all surfaces of items that belong elsewhere, discard all magazines and newspapers. Remember: It is not a sin to throw away old copies of *National Geographic.*

WHY: No matter how often you throw out this kind of stuff, there's always more to deal with.

Basket Tricks

For those of you who can't stand throwing away books and magazines, do as I do. Keep a basket of these near the door and invite guests, when leaving, to help themselves. Also keep a basket the exact size to hold newspapers so you can stack them for recycling.

WEEKLY

CLEAN LIGHT SWITCHES, GLASS TABLETOPS.

• Use all-purpose cleaner on a cloth to remove smudges.

WHY: Don't allow grime to accumulate. It gets harder to remove.

DUST DRAPES.

If you have a lot of drapes, do one section per week.

Drape Clusters

To get drapes out of the way when you're doing a thorough vacuuming, slip the ends through a hanger and hang it on the curtain rod or valance or other convenient spot.

DUST BLINDS, FURNITURE, PIANO, KNICKKNACKS.

• Refer to Dusting 101, p. 35, for instructions on using your feather duster and lambswool duster. (Note: To clean fabric or vertical blinds, you will need the vacuum cleaner dusting attachment instead.)

• Keep piano closed when not in use (unless you have real ivory keys, which will yellow away from light).

WHY: Don't allow dirt to accumulate. Move dirt to floor where it will be vacuumed.

VACUUM FLOOR.

• Vacuum high-traffic areas to remove visible cobwebs, dirt, and dust from the baseboards and spray with a cobweb eliminating spray.

WHY: Prevent dirt from being ground in, grime from accumulating—it's harder to clean.

Enough
∧

CLEAN LAMPS AND LAMPSHADES.

• Wipe bases with a damp cloth and vacuum shades.

WHY: As grime accumulates, lamps and shades get harder to clean.

VACUUM UPHOLSTERY.

• Vacuum upholstered furniture regularly using low-level suction. Frequency depends on how much use the furniture gets and how dirty the local air is. No one I know vacuums all the furniture each week, and you shouldn't either. My solution: Do one wall worth of furniture per week, and when the month's over, start again. Don't forget to vacuum under the cushions. Weird stuff accumulates there.

WHY: Same reason: Accumulated grime builds up, and the furniture will be harder to clean.

Since Dust You Must

If you wipe the TV and blinds with fabric softener sheets, they'll attract less dust.

MONTHLY
DUST BASEBOARDS.

• Use a lambswool duster.

WHY: Baseboards, one of the most ignored spots in the house, actually collect a tremendous amount of dust. The more you clean them, the more you will keep dirt from circulating in the house.

EVERY 6 MONTHS
WASH CURTAINS.

• Take down and wash. (Follow manufacturer's instructions. Almost always, they should be washed on the gentle cycle.)

WHY: If they get too dingy, it's impossible to get them clean.

CLEAN FLOOR THOROUGHLY.

- Do a major vacuuming. Pull out heavy furniture and get underneath. If you don't have sliders under the legs, slip a paper bag under each of them and the sofa will be easier to move. To vacuum the whole rug, divide it into sections and do it one "row" at a time.

WHY: If dust is trapped underneath and behind furniture, it becomes a breeding ground for moths and carpet beetles.

DEAL WITH HEATING/AIR-CONDITIONING SYSTEM.

- Change filters as required in air-conditioning units (or wash them in the dishwasher if possible) and replace filters or fabric softener sheets behind floor registers. (In summer, AC filters may need monthly changes.)
- Remove return air grille from forced-air heating system and vacuum both sides of the grille as well as the inside of the duct.

WHY: System will operate more efficiently. This should be done throughout the whole house, not just in the living room.

Time Saver

Dust the air conditioner grille with a soft cloth while the unit is running. That way, the dust will be sucked right into the filter.

Cover Up

If you have a window air-conditioning unit that needs to be covered up in winter, you can simply use some clear contact paper cut to fit. It will go on smoothly and stay on, and it's easily pulled off when you're going to put it back in operation.

MOVE THE PIANO.

- Pull out and vacuum behind an upright.

WHY: Accumulated dirt can make the instrument deteriorate.

Cord Control

Pull together a lot of cords anywhere in the house by using a ponytail holder with the double balls.

ANNUALLY OR EVERY 2 YEARS
CLEAN DRAPES AND/OR FABRIC BLINDS.
• May need professional cleaning. (But if you've vacuumed them regularly, this may never be necessary.)
WHY: When they get too dirty, they can't be cleaned properly.

WAX FLOORS.
• If not surface sealed, floors may need waxing.
WHY: Waxing protects the floor against grime that could be ground in and gives it a smooth surface that's easy to damp-mop.

Decide

AREA RUGS
See also Carpets, pp. 170–174.
• *Fur rugs:* Sometimes they are washable (just like their former owners)—but not always. If the backing will hold, sheepskin can be machine-laundered and air-dried. But unbacked fur rugs will shrink. Rub in unscented talc to freshen them, then vacuum, but for deep cleaning—or if the rug is valuable or old—you need a professional.

- *Kilims and other woven rugs:* Refresh in a dryer set on air only. Otherwise, because of the risk that the color might bleed, have them professionally cleaned.
- *Oriental rugs:* These should be professionally cleaned if they are valuable; otherwise, follow the instructions for cleaning wall-to-wall carpeting. Since the fringe on these rugs inevitably tangles, I had it professionally cut off and the edges bound. Next time, I'm buying rugs with short fringe.
- *Sisal, rush, and other natural floor coverings:* These rugs made from plant fiber (not the rugs made to resemble these) should be sealed by professionals, then just shaken out or vacuumed regularly. Hosing won't hurt them, but check the label before using any kind of detergent; also make sure these coverings are dried thoroughly before returned to use.
- *Washable area rugs:* These can be vacuumed, then washed on the driveway or deck or picnic table. Add a mild detergent or a cleaner made for delicate materials to a bucket of water. Hose down the area where you'll be washing the rug, then lay it down. Pour the solution onto the rug, use a cloth to work the cleaner into any dirty spots, then use the hose to rinse the rug. Water should run down the slope of the driveway or into the slats beneath the deck or table. Rugs will dry flat, without clothesline creases, if hung over two parallel lines.

ARTIFICIAL FLOWERS

- To some, these are clutter. But to me, they're must-haves. In the craft shop, I found a spray that cleans them and makes maintenance a breeze. (The home remedy is to put salt in a paper bag and pull them through it several times.)

Enough
∧

BLINDS, NONVERTICAL

- When they're soiled, lay towels on the floor or carpeting below the window, take down the blinds and lay them flat, and use all-purpose spray to loosen the dirt. Wipe away the loosened dirt with a damp towel, and use another clean towel to dry them off. Turn the blinds over and repeat this procedure. Rehang immediately. The key is to have plenty of clean towels so you're not just moving the dirt around.

- *Bamboo:* If the manufacturer permits the use of water, use the same procedure as above.

- *Fabric, pleated:* Spot-clean with a cloth or sponge dipped in a liquid dishwashing detergent and lukewarm water. Rinse the spot thoroughly.

- *Vinyl:* Use a cloth or sponge dampened in a solution of warm water and liquid dishwashing soap. Wipe dry. Or take them down, hang them from hooks on shower wall or immerse them in a bathtub lined with towels (so the tub won't scratch), and wash in soapy water. Lay them on towels in the tub, in the basement, or on the deck and close them. Spray with an all-purpose cleaner and wipe with a cloth, or scrub with a lambswool duster dipped in soapy water. Turn them over and repeat on the other side. Wipe with a clean, damp cloth; dry with a third cloth. So they will attract less dust, coat them with a commercial antistatic polish made for plastics.

- *Wood:* Do not clean with water, since dampness may cause slats to warp or discolor even if the wood has been sealed. Don't use abrasive solutions or solvents, either. If the environment is very dusty, use furniture polish that contains no wax to clean the blinds.

MY VIEWERS TIP ME OFF: Cleaning Blinds

Bring soiled blinds to a do-it-yourself car wash that has hooks on the wall where you can hang them. Clean off all dirt and grime using the high-pressure hoses to shoot hot water. Rinse and wipe or air-dry, leaving them hanging so tapes don't shrink.

The Missing Piece

Often miniblinds fall down because a small plastic piece of the bracket is lost. You can make a fine replacement by cutting an old credit card to the proper size (using the plastic piece that remains on the blind as a pattern). Even if you don't have a problem with miniblinds, this is a great solution to keep in mind for situations in which you need a small plastic part.

BLINDS, VERTICAL

- Take the blind down, put it on a flat surface, and clean as directed below, one vane at a time. See Don'ts for Vertical Blinds, next page.
- *Aluminum or PVC:* Clean with a cloth or sponge dipped in liquid dishwashing detergent mixed with cold or lukewarm water. Do not rinse (to minimize static electricity), but dry with a cloth towel to avoid water marks. Do not risk scratching or marring with abrasive or strong cleaning products.
- *Fabric:* Spot-clean with a cloth or sponge dipped in a liquid dishwashing detergent and cold or lukewarm water. Rinse the spot thoroughly. Upholstery cleaner may be acceptable for heavy stains. (Check with the manufacturer and always test for colorfastness in an inconspicuous spot.)

Enough
∧

DON'TS for Vertical Blinds
- Do not use hot water or a solvent cleaner.
- Do not soak. The vane will lose its sizing as well as its fire retardant and soil-repellent finishes.
- Do not machine-wash or -dry, dry-clean, wring, or crush.
- Do not hang or fold over a clothesline.

BOOKS
- Use an ostrich feather duster or lambswool duster when you notice a layer of dust.
- Bookworms or musty odor: Put the book in a sealed plastic bag in the freezer for a couple of days.

CANDLESTICKS
- Put the candlestick in the freezer and use a plastic scraper to remove excess wax. Then aim a hair dryer set to medium at the candlestick, waving it back and forth.
- Or to remove a small amount of wax, dip candlestick into hot water and peel wax off.
- Votive candles can be put in the freezer and the wax will pop right out.

CARPETS, WALL-TO-WALL AND LARGE RUGS
- If a rug is really old, it may look worse after it's cleaned, because all those worn and matted areas become more obvious. But most rugs look better. There are various ways to proceed:

    Powdered or foam cleaners: Sometimes worked in with a machine.

    Shampoos: Sprayed on or applied with a mop, brush, or rented applicator.

    Water extraction ("steam cleaning"): The machine is similar to the shampoo applicator but produces better results. It applies a combination of hot water and detergent, then vacuums it up. Whoever rents you the equipment can supply the detergent. I've recommended that you buy a small extraction cleaner for spot cleaning, but to do the entire rug you need to rent a large machine.

Dry cleaning: This is the newest method of carpet cleaning and it's quick. Vacuum the carpet, use a special scrubbing machine to apply a formula that loosens oily and greasy particles, then vacuum again. Since the process involves much less moisture than water extraction, the rug is clean and ready to go right away.

The latter two methods can be performed by you or by a professional. If you're going with a pro, get a recommendation, just as you would with a doctor. Not all professional services are the same quality, and your carpet is a big investment. One way to get a good recommendation: Call the fanciest carpet emporium in town and ask who does their work. And when you hire a pro, don't fall for other services they may try to sell you; ask for a cleaning and protective finish only. Wall-to-wall is cleaned in place, but area rugs are usually taken away to be worked on.

Odor Underfoot

Sprinkle baking soda on carpet that has an odor, leave for a few hours, then vacuum.

DO'S for Do-It-Yourself Rug Cleaning

- Move furniture out of the room, but if that's not possible, prevent rust marks by slipping small plastic bags onto each leg.
- Open the windows. (You need ventilation.)

(*continued*)

- Read and observe all cautions.
- Test for colorfastness.
- After cleaning, wipe off any foam that's left on furniture or walls and brush the damp pile in one direction with a soft brush or special "rake-type" finishing tool.
- Keep everyone and the dog off the carpeting until it's completely dry.
- Speed up the drying with a fan, heat, and/or air-conditioning to prevent shrinking, discoloring, and mildew.

How to Remove a Carpet Stain

1. Blotting is key to success. To pick up a messy job that includes solids, use your squeegee and a dustpan. Then use towels or, if you've got one, a small water extraction machine. Even after extraction, there will be some residue, so use disposable diapers or a supply of clean white towels to blot it up. (No colored towels; they might cause additional staining.) Blot, don't rub, since rubbing spreads the stain. Work from the outside of the stain inward. Don't use stain remover until the blotting is complete. (If you're in a situation where you don't have time to blot right away, you could try sprinkling cat box filler on the spill and vacuuming it up when carpet's dry. Then proceed with step 2.)

2. Pour on a little club soda and sponge it up. Many fresh stains can be treated this way. If that's not effective, go on.

3. Spot cleaning won't work if your rug has a protective coating, so before you apply any spot cleaner, squirt some liquid detergent on a very damp cloth, rub it into the soiled area, then blot it up. That alone may remove the stain.

4. If not, use one of the commercial cleaners I recommended at the front of the book. Read the label to see which is most appropriate for your particular stain. *Always* test a little bit in an inconspicuous spot. Or you can try one of the home remedies. See Home Remedies for Carpet Stains, next page.

5. If one stain removal technique doesn't work, before you try another

neutralize the area by mixing 1 tablespoon baking soda and ¼ cup water; rub a small amount of this into the spot, then blot it up.

6. Don't panic if the area where you've removed a stain appears to have changed color. A cleaned patch always looks lighter and brighter than the carpet around it. In time, the difference won't be so obvious.

7. Afterward: Remove any residue by rinsing the fibers with warm water. Dampen a clean cloth and blot the area. Do this two or three times. Then put another clean, dry towel on the spot and weight it down with books or bricks until the area dries. If you don't do this, a stain may return the following week or so. That's because the stain itself has penetrated right down into the rug and maybe even the backing, and the stain remover will have pulled it back up.

Home Remedies for Carpet Stains

After you've removed as much of the spill or stain as possible, and blotted repeatedly, these few home remedies may be worth a try—especially if you have no commercial carpet stain remover on hand.

- *Fruit stains:* Dampen spot with water, dump on table salt, rub in lightly. Let set for a few minutes, to allow salt to be rubbed into stain. Brush out and vacuum. Repeat until stain has gone.
- *Greasy stains:* While stain is wet, sprinkle with baking soda or baby powder, rub it in, let it dry. Then vacuum and use a grease removal product recommended for clothing.
- *Hairball and ink:* Rubbing alcohol may help.
- *Miscellaneous:* Windex (which contains ammonia and water) often does the trick on fresh stains, especially animal stains (but don't use it on wool rugs). So does a spritz of foamy shaving cream from an aerosol can (but try a test in a hidden spot to make sure rug color isn't affected). Or make a sudsy solution of liquid Tide laundry detergent and water. Brush only suds onto the spot, first vertically, then horizontally. Blot up excess liquid. Place a towel and a couple of heavy books on top of the spot to absorb moisture.

(*continued*)

• *Wine:* Sprinkle with salt or baking soda, leave until absorbed, then vacuum. Or pour a little club soda on spot, blot, repeat until stain is gone. Or use a little white wine to remove red wine, blot, repeat until stain is gone.

Other Carpet Problems

• *Burns:* Rub burns with dry steel wool. If you feel confident, trim the tufts. If you're even more confident, and you have some spare carpeting, cut away the burned spot, use it as a template, and cut a fresh piece of carpet to plug in the spot.

• *Crushed pile:* Lay a damp cloth on area and gently press with a hot iron.

• *Dented (from weight of furniture):* Use an ice cube on the spot.

• *Matted:* A wire pet brush will refresh it. If you have a lot of matted carpeting, call a janitorial supply house and get a carpet rake.

Pet Peeves

You may have to put up with some minor annoyances in return for the pleasure of your pet's company. Here are some solutions that should help.

• To keep drapes clean on the bottom in a household with pets, spray them with static spray. Pet hair won't collect.

• Use a dry sponge to pick up pet hairs from upholstery.

• To deal with the pet hairs all over the rug, mist it with diluted liquid fabric softener, let it dry, then vacuum. Damp-mop hard surfaces with some liquid fabric softener and water and you'll be able to pick up pet hairs too. The fabric softener cuts the static electricity.

CHANDELIER

• ✪ Hang an umbrella upside down from the chandelier, then spray the chandelier with a cleaner containing ammonia or your own mix of 1 part alcohol to 3 parts water in a spray bottle. Let liquid collect in the umbrella.

• If you feel that the crystals need heavier cleaning, put

on a pair of white cotton gloves, spray the crystals with window cleaner, and get to work. You can get into tiny grooves without putting fingerprints on everything.

- While you're at it, give the chandelier a shot of cobweb eliminating spray to keep the spiders away.

Spot Stopper
If you can reach the chandelier with a hair dryer, set it to medium hot, hold it 8 inches away, and wave it back and forth on the chandelier after you've sprayed to help the crystals dry quickly. This prevents spotting.

CHROME TABLE LEGS
- Rub them with a piece of smooth, damp aluminum foil, shiny side out. The foil will turn black, but the chrome will sparkle.

CURTAINS
See p. 102.

DRAPES
- If you must have your drapes, dust them off with the upholstery brush of your vacuum cleaner, working from top to bottom.
- Or give them a real freshening by taking them down and putting them into the dryer set on "air only" with a slightly damp bath towel and a couple of fabric softener sheets for 30 minutes.
- Very dirty drapes need professional cleaning.

Enough

∧

Getting Hooked

- If you are throwing your drapes into the dryer, you can leave the hooks on. Flip them in one direction and cover them with masking tape.
- If you're sending them out for cleaning, you will have to remove the hooks. As you do, mark the places where they should be inserted with pink nail polish. The polish will stay on during the cleaning process and make rehanging easier.

Wrinkle Remover

If drapes are wrinkled, spray them with a fine-mist plant sprayer as they hang and the wrinkles will fall out. Add some baking soda to the water and you'll freshen the drapes as well.

FIREPLACE

- For general maintenance, use a dry sponge or vacuum the brick.
- When brick tiles are very dirty, dip a brush in white vinegar and scrub quickly. Sponge immediately to absorb the moisture. But if your fireplace is made of very old brick, it may crumble under vigorous cleaning. Test a corner, and if there's a problem, just dust.
- Use an artgum eraser to clean smoke off stone (especially good on porous, rock-front fireplaces).
- After you've used artgum, you can do heavy-duty cleaning on smooth stone or brick fireplaces with ½ cup trisodium phosphate to 1 gallon water. Apply it with a sponge. This product is effective but strong. Follow the cautions and wear gloves and eye protection.
- Have the fireplace stone sealed so it will resist grease or oils or soot. (This is especially helpful if you'll be cooking in your fireplace.)
- *Marble:* For a marble cleaner and sealer, contact your local stone dealer or a janitorial supply house. Your

Hot Stuff

- Clean the smoky film off fireplace doors by rubbing the doors with ashes direct from the fireplace. Buff with another damp cloth and the glass will come clean.
- To prevent soot from settling all over the house, dampen fireplace ashes with a plant mister before cleaning them out. Then shovel the ashes into a box and cover them with wet newspapers.
- Rub a candle stub along the track of your fireplace screen to keep it sliding easily. Or give it a shot of WD-40.

Finishing Rules for Furniture

Most new furniture has a polyurethane finish, but be certain what you have and select the appropriate cleanup method. Try the following:

- Start by rubbing in a few drops of boiled linseed oil. (You have to buy boiled linseed oil. You don't boil your own.)
  If it absorbs, the finish is oil.
  If it beads up, it has a hard finish.
- If you know it has a hard finish, determine what kind by rubbing acetone over a spot, moving gently in a circle.
  If it sheds acetone like water, it's polyurethane.
  If it dissolves in 30 seconds, it's lacquer.
  Varnishes and shellacs turn sticky and gel-like after a minute or two.
- To determine if it's varnish or shellac, test it with a few drops of denatured alcohol.
  Shellac dissolves quickly in denatured alcohol.
  Varnish reacts slowly.

home store may have a product too. Many such specialty products tend to be available only locally or via the Internet.

FURNITURE, HARD-FINISH WOOD

- You can't clean furniture until you know how it's finished. If you're not certain, see the box above.

- For a polyurethane finish, cleaning is just a matter of wiping with a damp cloth and then a dry one.
- For nonpolyurethane finishes, there are three types of cleaning products: aerosols, liquids, or wax. As an experiment, put a small amount of any of these on a piece of glass and watch what happens over time. If (like most aerosols) it quickly evaporates, what's the point of using this stuff? If eventually it turns color, becomes sticky, or gets dirty, think of what it's doing to your furniture.
- *Aerosols:* Though easy to apply, if applied directly to the furniture rather than to a cloth, its solvents may damage the finish. Also, an aerosol spray often leaves an irreversible, slightly milky finish. You're better off with a clean, damp dustcloth—it won't cost you anything, and it won't do any harm.
- *Liquids:* These are either water- or oil-based and contain waxes, oils, detergents, and other ingredients. They may contain abrasives that can damage a surface. Since liquids tend to leave more product on the surface than aerosols, they can potentially be more damaging. There are two types of liquids:

    The nondrying oils (paraffin, mineral oil, and "lemon oil," which is usually just mineral oil with added color and fragrance) tend to leave a coating that attracts dust.

    The drying oils (linseed, tung, walnut oil) turn yellow and darken over time, and because of chemical changes also become increasingly hard to remove. They're better as a finishing product than as a polish.
- *Paste waxes:* These are actually semisolids. Many experts say these are the only choice for fine furniture— but be sure to choose a brand that does not contain silicone or acrylic resin, which seals the wood. Paste waxes take time to apply and buffing can be hard work, but wax fills in scratches and other surface

blemishes. Best of all, you hardly ever need to rewax—only once every 2 or 3 years for most surfaces, every 6 months or so for surfaces that get hard use. It's time to rewax when polishing with a cloth doesn't bring up a shine.

- If the surface of a piece of furniture is peeling, you may damage it if you clean, polish, or wax it. Either have it refinished or pretend it's an antique and just enjoy it as is.

FURNITURE, NONWOOD

- *Acrylic:* Cut down on dust—which it attracts like a magnet—by wiping with a fabric softener sheet, or use antistatic spray.
- *Black lacquer:* Polish with car wax. Buff to remove any excess.
- *Painted:* Clean it with a cloth dampened lightly with warm water and a very small amount of detergent. Or use Murphy Oil Soap—it's very gentle. Wring out the cloth and work on a small section at a time. Wipe, then dry. Any other product removes painted decorations. If the surface is peeling, just leave it be, or you may harm it.

    See also Upholstery, p. 185.

FURNITURE, OIL-FINISH WOOD

- *Dirty:* Mix 1 cup boiled linseed oil, 1 cup turpentine, and ⅓ cup white vinegar. (Observe all the cautions with turpentine: It's very flammable, it should not be breathed in, and you should wear rubber gloves.) Dip a cloth into the solution and apply it to the surface. Leave for a few minutes, then wipe away all excess so it won't attract dust. Buff, rubbing with the grain. It may look darker at first, but that's okay; eventually, the oil will be absorbed.
- *Dull:* Use a drying oil (boiled linseed or tung or man-

Enough
^

ufacturer's suggestion), not paraffin, mineral oil, or lemon oil, and never use wax. Apply the oil sparingly and infrequently or it will turn into a hard buildup.

• *Hard buildup:* If this occurs, dissolve the excess with mineral spirits or paint thinner. (Use the same cautions as for turpentine. Wash gloves with hot, sudsy water or get rid of them; cloths used for this procedure should be air-dried so solvent evaporates.)

"Dust is a protective coating for fine furniture."
—Mario Buatta, interior designer

Waxing Tools

• If you use dust-control spray, which is basically mineral oil, apply it to the cloth rather than to the surface of furniture. It may cause wax to streak.

• Here's a two-in-one. Use a terry cloth towel when you're waxing. Use one side to apply wax, the other as the buffing cloth.

• A singleton sock, slipped over your hand, can be used to apply wax to chair rungs.

Rx for Furniture Problems

Always rub with the grain.

If the furniture is valuable, go to a professional. The following are tried-and-true home remedies.

• *Alcohol (drinks/perfume/medication spills):* Wipe immediately, rub with oil (lemon, linseed, mineral, or salad). If that's not successful, make a paste of mineral oil and powdered pumice or rottenstone (from hardware store). Rub gently. Buff and wax.

• *Burns:* Rub a little mayonnaise into a small burn, let set, then wipe. Or use a wax stick from the hardware store or home center. Scrape away the charred finish, heat a knife blade and melt the stick over the blade, then drip into place and smooth with your finger.

Or make a paste of powdered pumice or rottenstone (from hardware store) and mineral oil. Rub gently. Buff and wax.

- *Candle wax:* Scrape it and then remove the residue with De-Solv-It. If the wax has gone through the finish, it may have left a permanent stain.
- *Food and grease:* Dampen a cloth with liquid detergent or Murphy Oil Soap and lukewarm water. Wipe area, dry, use wax coloring stick.
- *Mildew:* Brush off spores, preferably outside so you don't scatter them all over the house. Dampen a cloth with mild soap and wipe the item, then dry it in the sun. If mildew remains, sponge lightly with rubbing alcohol and rewipe with a damp cloth.
- *Miscellaneous stains:* Try mineral oil, lemon oil, or vinegar and water. Rub gently. Wipe dry. Rub with extra-fine steel wool. Use wax stick.
- *Scratches:* With all minor scratches, apply a light coat of white petroleum jelly and leave for 24 hours. Rub into wood and wipe away excess, then polish as usual. For larger scratches, as appropriate, apply any of the following with a small brush or a cotton swab, or use a wax stick.

Cherry: Fill scratches with a shoe polish in matching color or apply darkened iodine.

Ebony: Use black shoe polish, eyebrow pencil, or crayon.

Light finished furniture: On shiny finishes, try tan shoe polish.

Mahogany: Buff with brown paste wax or rub with matching wax crayon.

Maple: Mix equal amounts iodine and denatured alcohol.

Red mahogany: Iodine.

Teak: Rub gently with 0000 steel wool. Rub in equal amounts of linseed oil and turpentine.

(continued)

Walnut: Break a fresh, unsalted walnut or pecan in half and rub the scratch with the broken side of the nut.

• *White water rings:* Use a lubricant such as petroleum jelly or furniture wax and leave it alone for 8 hours.

Or rub nongel toothpaste into a cloth and rub the cloth into the spot, going with the grain.

Or rub in a paste of mayonnaise, salad oil, or butter and cigarette ashes. If the mark remains, sprinkle a cloth with a few drops of ammonia and rub gently and quickly in a circle.

KNICKKNACKS, CHINA OR GLASS

• Whenever possible, don't clean them individually. Put them in the dishwasher if you have an adjustable temperature control and/or a fine-china cycle, which has a more gentle spray and runs for a brief amount of time.

• Or hand-wash them in a bunch. Lay a towel in a large pot, plastic container, or baking dish, put it in the sink or tub, and put the items inside, giving them a soak in soapy water, then rinse.

• Or put them outdoors and use the fine mist spray on your garden hose. Air-dry or point a hair dryer at them.

• Items too delicate to be washed can be cleaned with an artist's sable paintbrush #2 or #4. The long handle lets you get to hard-to-reach places, and the little brush allows you to work carefully.

LAMPSHADES

• Use a dry sponge or a microfiber cloth. Use a paintbrush to clean the pleats in pleated shades.

• Avoid spot cleaning, which will stain and/or remove the flame-resistant coating on many shades.

• The manufacturer's care label should indicate whether or not a shade can be washed.

Linen and cotton shades generally cannot be washed. Plastic-coated, laminated, parchment, or fiberglass shades (but not with glued-on trim or a painted design) can be washed: Put a little mild liquid detergent into a bowl that has a cover, add some water, cover the bowl, and shake it up to create suds. Using a terry cloth towel, apply suds only to the shade. Use another terry cloth towel to apply clean water. Apply only a minimum of liquid. Remove all soap residue, which attracts extra dirt. Dry thoroughly any metal portion of the shade to prevent rust, and let the shade air dry.

Silk, rayon, or nylon shades (unless they have a glued-on trim or a painted design) can go right into a soapy bath. Use a sponge or cloth to rub them gently. Drain the soap suds, and repeat if the shades are very dirty. Then immerse the shades in clean water to rinse, also repeating until water runs clear or leftover soap will attract more dirt. Fabric may look stretched out, but as it dries, it will tighten up. To prevent rust, dry thoroughly any metal portion of the shade. Use a string to hang the lampshade from its middle so it can drip-dry over the tub or from a clothesline.

PIANO

- I bought a piano when my career took off, thinking I'd take piano lessons. I didn't make the connection that once my career took off, I wouldn't have the time for piano lessons. Then I had the piano electrified, thinking that a player piano would be fun at parties, but I discovered unless you have palace-size rooms, the piano drowns out all the conversation. So if anyone's interested, I have a piano for sale. Fortunately, it doesn't require much attention.
- New piano cabinets require just occasional wiping with a dry or damp cloth and possible waxing with a

Enough
^

water-based solvent. Do not use an aerosol spray. Older cabinets may need occasional but not frequent polishing with a high-quality paste wax. Your piano tuner should vacuum out dust annually. If you have a valuable or antique piano, follow the manufacturer's instructions.

• Keeping the keyboard covered prevents dust, but ivory keys need sunlight or they'll turn yellow. Today, though, most keys are made of plastic (usually acrylic). Vacuum dust from between the keys. Wipe the keys with a cloth dampened with a mild liquid detergent and water for stubborn stains. Never use chemicals or solvents.

PICTURES

• *Frame:* Apply cleaners to the cloth, never directly to the glass or frame, so that liquid doesn't seep inside and stain the mat or artwork. Use a dry soft cloth on a gold- or silver-leafed frame or waxed wood, a cloth dampened with water on a sealed finish wood frame, and a cloth dampened with glass cleaner on a metal frame.

• *Glass:* Use a glass cleaner sprayed on a cloth; for Plexiglas, use a soft cloth and a Plexiglas cleaner. Or use eyeglass cleaning tissues or treated eyeglass cloth to clean glass on small pictures.

Dealing with a Hangup

To mount a picture on wallpaper without damaging it, cut a small V in the paper where each nail will be placed. Carefully lift the paper and hammer the picture-hanging nail directly into the Sheetrock. If you want to remove the picture, remove the nail, place craft glue on the flap of paper, and smooth the V back into place.

TABLETOPS

- *Glass:* Use commercial glass cleaner or add a capful of liquid fabric softener to a quart of water for a cleaner that will resist dust. If the item is glass and wood, take care not to get the glass cleaner on the wood, as it may leave a water stain. Dry dishwasher detergent will get water rings off a glass table.
- *Plexiglas:* Use special Plexiglas polish. For small scratches, gently rub in nongel toothpaste, then buff.
- *Granite:* For regular cleaning, just use a damp cloth.

   Heat stain: If there is a stain caused by heat, the surface was probably improperly sealed. Talk to your manufacturer.

   Water stain: Usually shows up as a dark spot. Place some dry flour on the spot and let it sit overnight. If there is moisture, the flour should dry it out.
- *Leather:* See p. 189.
- *Marble:* See pp. 75–77.

UPHOLSTERY

- *Fabric:* My best advice for upholstery cleaning is this: (1) choose a fabric that's practical for your use (see The Good Enough Housekeeper's Guide to Choosing Upholstery Fabrics, p. 160); and (2) protect it. Do not use the sofa as a dining table and keep the cat and dog off it (see Critters off the Couch, p. 187). Blot up spills as soon as they happen (and blot and blot and blot again), and use a spot-removing product right away.
- Many manufacturers have adopted a standard code that lets you know how to clean your furniture. Find the label on the fabric sample, on the furniture cushion, or on the tag hanging from the furniture. Here are the code letters and what they mean.

   W: Use a water-based cleaner. Before you use it, though, test for shrinkage, fading, bleeding, and residue in a hidden area (see Test Run, p. 187).

- By hand: Add 1 teaspoon of detergent (such as Tide) to 1 quart of water, shake it up, and use the foam. Avoid soaking the furniture so you don't cause a mildew problem. Apply only a small amount, then apply a damp sponge with clean water, then blot. Or use commercial upholstery shampoo, following the directions. The type that comes in an aerosol can is least likely to saturate the furniture. Put a fan in front of the furniture to speed up the drying.
- By machine: Use an extraction cleaner. See Carpets, pp. 170–174, for more details about extraction cleaning. It is critical that you don't oversaturate the furniture.

S: Use a solvent-based cleaner. Water stains this kind of fabric. Basically, you're limited to spot cleaning. (Having an entire item of furniture cleaned with a solvent can be done only by a pro.) For spot cleaning, use a solvent-containing powder that you brush on and then vacuum up or a dry-cleaning solvent (like Carbona or Energine). Observe the cautions on the label about flammability and ventilation. Apply with a terry cloth, wipe with another terry.

S–W: Use either of the methods described above. Food stains usually require a water-based cleaner; grease and oil need one that is solvent-based.

X: Nothing but vacuuming or light brushing. Otherwise this item may shrink, fade, or spot.

The Biggest Upholstery-Cleaning Mistake

Do NOT assume that the zipper around the cushions that match your sofa or chair is a sign that you can remove the cover and launder or dry-clean it. I can almost guarantee that the cover will shrink and/or turn a color that doesn't match the furniture. The zipper is there only so that the cover can be slipped over the stuffing.

Test Run

Before you use any upholstery cleaner, check for the following.

- *Shrinkage:* Apply a bit of the cleaning solution in a hidden spot. If the fabric dries tighter or pulls together, this product causes shrinkage.
- *Colorfastness:* Apply the cleaning solution to a white rag and press it on a hidden spot. If the color bleeds, the only acceptable cleaner is a dry-cleaning solvent, for spot cleaning only. Otherwise send it to the pros.
- *Residue:* Apply the cleaning solution and allow to dry. If the area is sticky, choose another cleaning solution. Or make sure to sponge away residue after you have cleaned because it will quickly attract more dirt.
- Also, if cushions contain latex foam rubber, don't use a dry-cleaning solvent.
- If stuffing threads in the sofa cushion are dark-colored or cushions are stuffed with jute, it can't get wet or it may turn the material brown. Apply the product with damp sponge, wringing it out in clear water, and repeating. Work a small area at a time and use very little liquid.

Critters off the Couch

One or another of these tricks may help to keep Fluffy or Fido off the furniture:

- Covering the cushion with a sheet of foil may train the cat not to go up there. She won't like the crackle.

(*continued*)

- Landing on an inflated balloon on the sofa may teach your cat or dog a lesson to remember.
- Use a squirt gun to zap a cat who is scratching the couch (or jumping on the table). He'll stay away.
- Cats will stay away from a furniture leg that's been wiped with chili sauce and blotted thoroughly. You won't be able to smell it, but your pet will. Many also hate the odor of liniment (such as Bengay), and dogs will stay away from oil of cloves, either of which can also be applied to a furniture that's sealed.
- If all else fails, put a washable throw on the couch and hope your pet will use that as his "bed."

DO'S for Upholstery Stain Removal

- As with carpeting, there are few home remedies that are really effective, and most work only when you deal with the stain right away. Blot up as much of the stain as you can before you try to clean it. You'll need either a dry-cleaning solvent, which you should have on hand (and test before use; see Test Run, p. 187), or a solution involving water. Do not saturate any spot you're treating or you may wind up with both the spot and a new problem—mildew. Also, dry the furniture as quickly as possible. Use a fan, a heater, or air-conditioning to help the process along.
- *Lipstick, other greasy stains:* Dry-cleaning solvent. Follow directions on label.
- *Small, nongreasy stains:* Mix I teaspoon liquid dishwashing detergent in 2 cups water, shake it up, and apply suds only. Apply a small amount and blot between applications.
- *Chocolate, coffee with cream, and other combination stains:* First use the detergent solution described in the paragraph above, then the solvent.

    Because you're working from one side only, you're always driving the stain into the filling. If you have no success, call in a professional who has been recommended to you. But even the good ones won't make your couch look brand-new again—especially if it's badly soiled or stained.

- *Leather:* Consult the manufacturer to find out how the finish on your leather furniture has been treated.

  Coated leather can be cleaned, and stains can be removed, with just a damp cloth. Coated leather won't darken when exposed to moisture. Or use a dilute solution of the mildest cleaner (such as Ivory Snow or Neutrogena). Apply gently, using a terry glove or gentle net scrubber or exfoliating glove to get the dirt out of the grooves. If soil remains, then dye has transferred or dirt has been ground in. Remove soap residue with another damp cloth.

  Uncoated leather is easily stained by furniture polish among other substances. If it is grimy, get advice from the manufacturer. Usually, it is safe to clean it with saddle soap, a mild soap good for cleaning and softening leather.

VASES

- Remove a stain from the bottom of a vase by filling it with water and dropping in a couple of denture tablets.
- To get suds out of a long-necked bottle or carafe after washing, add a few drops of liquid fabric softener to a small amount of water in the bottle, then swish it out.

WINDOWS

Believe me, I've tried dozens of window-cleaning techniques. This is the very best one of all. While many people advise against using a lot of soap, in this method you use lots: The soap is what makes the squeegee glide smoothly against the glass.

- Before you start, remove any spotting (from tree sap, hard water, or bird droppings). Wet the spots down

Enough
∧

and scrape them away with a safety razor, keeping the surface continually damp to avoid scratching. To remove any gummy residue, use Goo Gone or De-Solv-It.

• Then gather the window-washing equipment: a couple of Ettore window squeegees in sizes that work for your windows, an Ettore window scrubber (a clothlike applicator on a squeegee-type handle), a couple of terry towels, and lemon-scented dishwashing liquid (because acid in the lemon helps cut through grime).

• You also need a three-compartment cleaning caddy with a handle. Two compartments will hold the squeegee and scrubber, and one will hold the cleaning solution. (Carry the cloths around your neck or over your arm.)

1. Squirt three 10-inch-long squirts of the liquid into the long, narrow section of the caddy and add about 2–3 inches of water.

2. Dip the scrubber in the solution, and squeeze it out so it's not dripping. Apply the thick, sudsy solution to the window. (You will probably have enough solution on the scrubber to apply to several windows without redipping it.)

3. Using the dry squeegee blade, take a horizontal swipe across the top of the window. With a towel, dry the uppermost part of the pane so no water is dripping down.

4. Then, putting the blade on a dry part of the glass, begin cleaning the window vertically. Always dry your blade in between swipes.

• If there is any streaking, allow it to air-dry, but wipe the base and the sides of the window with a cloth.

I think this method has cut my cleaning time in half. Even if you have to hire a professional to clean any of your windows that are difficult to reach, try this technique on the ones that are accessible. You'll find it's a winner.

Tips for Cleaning a Window

- Hold the squeegee at an angle to the glass, not straight.
- Don't clean when the sun's beating down: The quick evaporation of water causes streaks.
- Clean the tracks with a small foam paintbrush, or spray the cleaner onto a piece of cloth wrapped around a pencil. If there's additional debris, clean it out with your wet vac.

Mending a Crack

Need a temporary repair for a broken window? Use silicone rubber aquarium sealer. It will prevent drafts and further cracking, and it's an inexpensive solution.

WINDOW SCREENS

- Use the dusting attachment of a vacuum cleaner or brush with carpet scraps that have been nailed to a wooden block before you clean. Or use a dry sponge.
- When they're visibly grimy, wash screens outdoors (preferably) or on the basement floor. If you are washing them in the tub, line it with towels so it won't be scratched. Wash one side of the screen with soapy water and sponge it off, then turn to other side and repeat. Or spray foaming bathroom cleaner on the screen, leave for 10 minutes, gently brush, then rinse with hose or shower.
- Brush both sides of a metal screen with kerosene and wipe with a clean cloth to prevent rust.

MY VIEWERS TIP ME OFF
I've been told that you can take very, very dirty screens to a do-it-yourself car wash that has hooks on the wall where you can hang them. Let the high-pressure hoses shoot streams of hot, soapy water to clean off all the dirt and grime.

Screen Gem
As a temporary patch for a hole in a window screen, use Scribbles Glittering Silver paint that's used to decorate T-shirts. It's the same color as the screen.

Floor Finishes
- Some wood floors are treated with a penetrating sealer that is allowed to soak into the wood. When it hardens, it protects the floor against dirt and stains. A layer of wax is added as a final protection.
- Surface-finished floors—urethanes and polyurethanes—are topped with a film that is very resistant to spills and splashes, so that it can be used even in the kitchen of the sloppiest cook.
- Sometimes people cover a waxed floor with a surface sealer, but you can't do the reverse. Waxing a surface-sealed floor makes it slippery, water spots become more obvious, and dirt will become embedded in the finish and wear it away. But the real argument against it is that it's a lot more work!
- If you're not sure what kind of floor you have, drip two drops of water in a hidden area. If white spots form within 10 minutes, the floor is waxed. (Those white spots will go away if you rub them with 000 steel wool dampened with wax.)
- Floors dating back to the mid-60s or earlier may be shellacked or varnished. To test: Use a sharp tool to make a scratch in a hidden

area; if you see flaking, you've probably got shellac or varnish. This floor should probably be sanded down and refinished.

WOOD FLOOR, SURFACE-FINISHED, STAIN REMOVAL AND OTHER PROBLEMS

- Treat bleached wood as other surface-finished floors. Because of its light color, it may need more frequent cleaning.
- When the weather is dry or the heat is on, the floor will contract and dark lines between flooring strips will be very noticeable. The situation will resolve itself when the weather changes.
- *Chewing gum, crayon, wax:* Wave a hair dryer set on warm at the area until the wax melts, then blot it up. Remove any residue with the edge of a credit card or other dull scraping tool. Clean the area with a product made for urethane finishes.
- *Cigarette burns:* Get a touch-up kit for urethane finishes from a wood-flooring dealer. Usually this involves sandpapering, staining, and refinishing. If the burn is deep, a section of a board or the entire board may need to be replaced.
- *Protein or grease stains:* Buy a cleaner made for urethane. If you can't live with good enough and want to repair this floor yourself, you can sand to the bare wood, apply some stain as close to the color as you can find, then wipe on semigloss varnish. Use a lint-free cloth to apply very little, let dry, and repeat multiple times if necessary. The risk is in applying polyurethane varnish to an unknown finish. Some polyurethanes are not compatible with others, but an oil-based polyurethane is the best bet.
- *Scratches:* Get a touch-up kit made for urethane finishes from a wood-flooring retailer.

WOOD FLOOR, WAX FINISH, CLEANING

- A wood floor that's waxed (see Floor Finishes, p. 192) usually needs rewaxing once a year. Self-polishing waxes meant for vinyl or tile make wood slippery and dull. Instead, stick with a solvent-based wax that will strip off old wax and apply new wax in one step. Check with the manufacturer of your floor to see if there's a recommended brand or type.
- *Easiest:* Self-polishing liquids (e.g., Wood Preen, Bissell One Step) are a cinch to apply and don't need buffing.
- *Longest-lasting:* Paste wax. Best when applied by hand, with a cloth, or with a non-electric applicator. Wait 15 minutes, then use a machine to buff it.
- *Best compromise:* Buffable liquid wax. Let wax dry several hours before you buff. Here's a little trick: Dry floors quickly with a portable fan set at one end of the room. Machine application may be a problem (wax may clog it and it doesn't lay the wax down evenly), but machine buffing is easy.

WOOD FLOOR, WAX FINISH, STAINS, AND MARKS

- In stain removal, always scrub from the outside in.
- *Alcohol:* Rub with cloth barely dampened with ammonia.
- *Chewing gum, candle wax, crayon:* Point a hair dryer at the surface until gum is soft or until other substances can be blotted up, or put down a brown paper bag that has no printing on top and iron over that, using a fresh portion at a time until all the wax is absorbed. Or put a bag of ice on the area until the wax is brittle enough to be scraped off with a plastic credit card.
- *Cigarette burns:* On a shallow burn, use fine sandpaper, or dampen steel wool with solvent-based wax, rub

onto area with clean cloth, buff. On a deeper burn, use a scraping tool to remove charred area. Use fine sandpaper, then stain, wax, and hand-buff.

- *Darkening in well-worn area (such as under a rocking chair):* Dampen fine steel wool with mineral spirits and rub. Remove all residue before applying new wax.
- *Dent:* Strip floor of wax, polish, dirt, and anything else that would interfere with adhesion of any compound. Lay a damp cloth or several layers of brown paper bags over the spot and run a warm iron over it. Wood fibers will swell and rise up. If not, put a gallon jug filled with very hot water on the spot for half an hour, then pick it up and lay down the cloth or paper bags and iron again.
- *Dried milk or food stains:* Rub with a damp cloth, dry, then wax.
- *Dull:* If a single spot is dull, rub it with a piece of waxed paper or do a touchup with a one-step or buffable wax such as Wood Preen or Bissell One Step, following instructions on the container. If the whole floor is dull and buffing won't make it shine, it needs rewaxing. If it is dull and also slippery, you may have used too much wax; try buffing alone. If, however, you used a polish that wasn't suitable for wood floors, you may need an extreme solution such as sanding and refinishing.
- *Gouge:* Strip the area—ideally, a single plank—of wax, polish, dirt, or anything that would prevent a compound from adhering to the surface. Use a wood-patching wax stick. Then rewax.
- *Heel marks:* Rub in a small amount of wax with fine steel wool and hand-buff to a shine.
- *Hole:* For a problem too big to qualify as a dent or a gouge, use plastic wood or wood putty. Overfill, because these compounds shrink when dry. Sand it flat

with a piece of wood larger than the hole, and cover with a stain. Or cut a patch from another piece of wood, use plastic wood to fill any cracks, and then stain everything to match. Coat with wax, then buff.

- *Ink stains:* Treat as urine stains.
- *Mold:* Use special wood cleaner meant to kill mildew.
- *Mystery spot:* Dampen fine steel wool with odorless mineral spirits. Then wash area with vinegar, let stand 3–4 minutes, and wipe with mineral spirits. Sand with fine sandpaper, "feathering" out 3–4 inches all around. Stain, rewax, and repolish.
- *Oil and grease stains:* Saturate a cotton ball with 3% hydrogen peroxide and place it over the stain. Then saturate a second layer of cotton with ammonia and place over the first. Repeat until the stain is removed. Let the area dry, then hand-buff.
- *Scratches:* Wax the area.
- *Urine stains:* Try the water stains treatment. If the spot remains, you'll have to remove the color and re-stain. Call in a professional, or take your chances and apply bleach or vinegar to the spot, leaving it for an hour. Use a damp cloth to rinse the liquid away, dry, and sand with fine sandpaper. Reapply stain, wax, and hand-buff.
- *Water stains or white spots:* Dip 0000 steel wool in wax, then rub with the grain. If that isn't satisfactory, use fine sandpaper, rubbing lightly, then clean the spot with 00 steel wool and mineral spirits or a wood floor cleaner. Allow the floor to dry. Stain, wax, and hand-buff.
- *Worn:* If the floor is very worn, it will probably require professional refinishing. But you can touch up spots with a little brown shoe polish added to liquid floor wax. The polish makes it look antiqued.

Floor Protection

- Put mats or area rugs at entrances so dirt isn't tracked in.
- Since sunlight can bleach dark wood, use blinds (or drapes, if you must) where possible to block the sun. Or use area rugs for protection.
- Use casters on furniture, but choose rubber ones, not plastic.
- Under chairs and tables, however, use nonrubber glides, little disks that attach with adhesive, nails, or screws.
- Sports shoes, cleats, and stiletto heels are the enemy of floors. An elephant's foot exerts 50–100 pounds of pressure per square inch, a 125-pound lady's heel up to 2,000, an exposed nail in the heel up to 8,000. Many floor warranties don't cover damage from heels, so put new heels and toes on your shoes as needed.

WOOD PANELING

- Remove soil with a dry sponge or apply Murphy Oil Soap following instructions on bottle.
- Either a Sh-Mop or a Swiffer, wet or dry, is a great tool for cleaning hard-to-reach paneling.

TWELVE

The Patio Furnishings, Garage, Driveway, and Basement

> **Good enough housekeeping** is cutting back your cleaning problems by cutting back on stuff you own.

The secret to easy cleaning of the basement and garage is to keep them as empty as possible. And the secret to cutting down on patio equipment care is choosing the right stuff. Backyards are meant for relaxing, not for work.

Dejunk

The garage and basement are prime locations for clutter. I know all the tricks and rationales you use to hang on to this stuff, and none of them are good enough. Do whatever's necessary (bribes, threats, or guilt treatments) to get family help in doing a big cleanout. Most basement and garage cleaning problems are due to overaccumulation.

DO'S for the Backyard, Garage, Driveway, and Basement

- Use a low-maintenance product for your decking, such as composite decking made from wood products (sawdust) and resins. Available at most building supply stores, it costs a little more than wood (about $2 a linear foot), but since upkeep is minimal, it's a better deal in the long run. It's also strong and splinter free.

- Do not buy chairs, tables, cushions, or anything else for your yard that can't be left outdoors at all times. In Minnesota where I live, winters are tough, but my garden furniture is tougher. I just throw a cover on it, and come spring, it's ready to go.

- To protect the hammock when there's a rainstorm, buy a twin-sized plastic mattress cover that you can fasten with clothespins. (A cover expressly for this purpose, if you can find one, is expensive.)

- Buy a pressure washer. As I said at the beginning of this book, in a fraction of the time you'd otherwise spend, this tool can clean anything in your yard, including bricks, stone, and siding on the house. I even take it onto the roof to blow off moss. You'll more than make up its cost by not having to buy a lot of other cleaning products, hire professional cleaning services, or replace items that this equipment can help you maintain.

- Seal your basement and garage floors. Once the concrete is sealed, spills are much less problematic because they won't stain. There's a concrete stain on the market that won't peel.

- Put down rubber-backed carpeting in the garage under the car and all the way to the door to pick up any debris that might otherwise be tracked inside.

- Get stuff off the ground and better organized in the garage. Add

(continued)

shelf space in a jiffy using just four lengths of chain and eight S-hooks. Fasten four of the hooks to the shelf corners and the other four to the ceiling or beam above.

• No matter where you store anything in a garage, don't leave it in the box. Boxes get wet and fall apart. Transfer everything to plastic containers.

• Do yourself the biggest favor in the world and never finish a basement until you're absolutely, positively sure it's waterproof. When you move into a new house, wait until you go through a horrible rainstorm without any leaks. Even so, have it thoroughly inspected before you proceed. Thanks to new building codes, floods are less common than they used to be, but it's better to be safe than sorry.

Defend

THE BASIC SUPPLIES FOR GOOD ENOUGH PATIO, DECK, DRIVEWAY, AND BASEMENT CLEANING

All-purpose cleaner or mild detergent and cloth
Pressure washer
Possibly: sealer/paint for wood furniture

DAILY
TAKE FURNISHINGS INDOORS.

• Bring urethane-filled cushions and any others that aren't completely weatherproof inside at night/when it rains.

WHY: Prevent mildewing.

• Bring metal furniture in at night/when it rains.

WHY: Rust spots may develop on furniture and the patio or deck.

CLEAN VINYL-STRAPPED FURNITURE.

- Just wipe; or use all-purpose cleaner or mild detergent and water to remove dirt, oil, and suntan lotion. If you need a little extra scrubbing power, sprinkle baking soda or vinegar on a terry cloth towel, wipe, and then use the cleaner.

WHY: Prevent fungus that rots straps.

PROTECT VINYL FURNITURE AND COVERED CUSHIONS.

- Drape them with towels.

WHY: Combination of sun and suntan lotion and oil may stain. Also see below.

Vinyl and Bleach

Bleach destroys the finish on vinyl. So never come out of the pool and sit down on any vinyl furniture without first covering it with a towel. And since pool chlorine is much stronger than household bleach, don't be tempted to throw this kind of furniture in the pool to clean it. But as the vinyl finish wears away, and the furniture becomes more vulnerable to soiling, it's okay to add a little bleach to the all-purpose cleaner to get it clean. Start with a capful in the bucket and up the quantity as needed. By the time you start to need a lot, the vinyl straps will be fading anyway. Alternatively, use automobile vinyl cleaner.

SEASONALLY
SEAL NONWOOD FURNITURE.

- Plastic, aluminum, and metal need weatherproofing.
- Use two thin coats of auto wax on painted metal; clear liquid on textured metal.

WHY: Protects against pitting (plastic and aluminum) and rust (metal).

PAINT WICKER.

• Use marine varnish if you'll be using it outdoors

WHY: Will deteriorate when exposed to elements.

DEEP-CLEAN NONWATERPROOF CUSHIONS.

• Unless the manufacturer cautions against the use of bleach, mix 1 cup chlorine bleach, 1 cup powdered laundry detergent, and 3 gallons water. Don't pour bleach directly on cushions. Put cushions in tub to soak for half an hour or saturate them and leave them on cement or patio. Rinse thoroughly, then dry several days in sun.

WHY: To kill any mildew.

COVER FURNITURE SEASONALLY.

• Protect wrought and cast (solid) iron and casual (hollow) aluminum.

WHY: All are prone to rusting.

CLEAN THE UMBRELLA.

• Umbrellas that look and feel like canvas are usually made of synthetic acrylic today. Put the weighted bottom of the umbrella on the ground, then slip the top portion only (not the extension pole) into it so that you can extend the umbrella and easily reach down to clean any part. Hose off superficial dirt, sponge-clean with dishwashing detergent and water or an auto vinyl-top cleaner, then hose again. Use a sponge rather than a scrub brush on acrylics or any fabrics with a raised weave to avoid pilling.

• Mildew won't grow on the synthetic fibers that new umbrellas are made of but may grow on any dirt left in the umbrella. If you see those telltale black spots, unless the manufacturer says no bleach, pour ¼ cup bleach in a 32-ounce spray container, fill it with water, and spray the solution. After a few minutes, hose it off or treat stubborn spots with a sponge.

WHY: Prevent deterioration.

Foot Notes

When you're running in and out from the garden, you can track a lot of dirt inside, but having a good mat at the door cuts down on the problem. In addition:

- Leave a pair of rubber clogs or other shoes you can easily slip in and out of in a basket by the door. (You can also keep a pair of shears for cutting flowers and other tools handy in the basket.)
- Or leave a couple of disposable shower caps by the door to slip right over laced-up shoes if you're making a quick trip outside on a snowy or muddy day.

AS NEEDED

ANTICIPATE BASEMENT WATER DAMAGE.

- Use a dehumidifier.
- Use carpeting that isn't glued down but can be picked up to dry.
- Never store anything directly on the floor.
- Replace cardboard storage boxes with plastic containers.

WHY: Even if natural elements don't flood your basement, there's always the danger of a leak.

PAINT/SEAL WOOD FURNITURE.

- Check with the manufacturer to see how often treatment should be repeated. May be as infrequently as every 3–5 years or more depending on what paint/sealer you choose.

WHY: Moisture getting in cracks will cause the furniture to deteriorate.

Trash Talking

- If you don't have a shed for your garbage pails, drive a pole into the ground and slip the handle over it to prevent the cover from being blown away and the can from tipping over.
- Put bricks or other items under the can to lift it off the ground and drill holes underneath so liquid can drain off—making less weight when you have to drag the can to the curb.
- If one rubber can is stuck inside another, jam the hose down inside the bottom one and pour in a bit of dish soap. When water fills the bottom can, the top one will begin to lift out.

Decide

ALUMINUM FURNITURE

- Painted aluminum can be cleaned with hot, soapy water; grimy spots can be removed with baking soda.
- If furniture is discolored and pitted, use steel wool pads, but rinse thoroughly because leftover bits of steel can cause staining. Or use naval jelly from the auto supply store.

Save a Seat

Keep old metal furniture from rusting by drilling a few small holes in the seats for water to drain through.

Fancy Footwork

Plastic caps from 2-liter soft drink containers are about the right size to slip over tabular aluminum furniture feet, so they don't dig into the grass.

AWNING

- If your awning is made of vinyl fabric (as most are today), it usually contains PVC, which is petroleum based, so don't use a degreaser or any cleaner containing alcohol or solvent. A mild detergent is okay, but if you have very grimy awnings, check with the manufacturer.
- Canvas awnings are usually made of synthetic fibers that look like canvas. Use a mild detergent to avoid color bleeding. Wet canvas may continue to appear dingy, so judge results only when it's dry.

BARBECUE GRILL, KETTLE-STYLE

- Clean out the ashes from under the grates. Remove the grill and the charcoal grates, spray the inside of the grill with oven cleaner spray, then return the grates to their usual position and spray them, too. Leave overnight or for the amount of time recommended on the can, then remove grates, lay them on newspaper, and use a steel wool pad, grill brush, or plastic scrubber (if grates are nonstick) to clean off debris. Wipe inside grill with crumpled newspaper. Hose down the grates and the grill.
- Or get the grill very, very hot, then dip a long-handled 2-inch metal brush in water and stroke it over the grill. The water will "steam clean" the grill and you won't have to do nearly as much scrubbing.

Enough
∧

• Or seal the grates in a plastic bag overnight with a cup of ammonia. When you open the bag, point it away from your face. Proceed as above with steel wool or a plastic scrubber.

Oil's Well

Spray nonstick vegetable oil on the grate before you start cooking and it will be much easier to clean.

Icy Brick Road

Deicers on your brick patio will cause it to deteriorate. Instead use sand (without salt) or cat box filler to provide traction during icy winter months.

CANE

• Just wipe with a damp cloth.

Get a Grip

Mix 1 part sand to 4 parts paint when you're painting steps or deck; they'll be less slippery.

CONCRETE DRIVEWAY/GARAGE FLOOR

• Being porous, concrete stains easily. Once a stain is removed, use an all-purpose cleaner. If it's a garage floor, seal it.
• *Mold:* Sponge-mop with a mixture of 1 part bleach and 4 parts water. Apply rinse water with a stiff broom. (This mixture may harm grass; be careful when applying it.) Or use a mildewcide sold for use around swimming pools.
• *Oil drips:* Sprinkle with cat box filler or granulated dishwasher detergent; or use sweeping compound that absorbs grease (may be purchased at your local service station or janitorial supply center). Leave overnight, then sweep or vacuum away.

• *Grease stains:*

Spray on prewash spray, let it stand 5 minutes, then sprinkle on powdered detergent, scrub with a broom or hose off.

Or mix 1 part trisodium phosphate with 6 parts of water and as much lime as needed to make a thick paste. Spread a ¼-inch layer of the paste over the stained areas and leave until it is thoroughly dry. Remove. Then scrub with clear water. (Caution: This can be toxic to surrounding greenery.)

Or spray on oven cleaner, let set 15 minutes, hose off. (Caution: This can be toxic to surrounding greenery.)

• *Rust:*

Sprinkle on portland cement (a powder used in making concrete), then sprinkle water on top and work cement into stain with a stiff push broom. Then rinse.

Or use a commercial rust remover.

Or use a pressure cleaner.

CUSHIONS

• Most cushions today are stuffed with polyester and made of synthetics, polyacrylics that feel like cotton or woven polyesters coated with polyvinyl chloride. They can be sponge-cleaned with detergent and water, then rinsed with a hose. However, cushions made of other fabrics and/or stuffed with urethane foam are susceptible to mildew and must be taken inside when it rains.

• Mildew won't grow on the acrylic covering but may grow inside the cushion. Unless the care tag warns against bleach, if the cushion smells musty, use a mixture of 1 part bleach to 2 or 3 parts soapy water, or use a mildew-removing bathroom product. Scrub if necessary, then rinse thoroughly with water.

Enough
∧

- To clean real canvas cushions, add about ½ cup liquid detergent to a gallon of water and scrub dirty canvas clean. Or rub on naphtha soap with a stiff brush. Hose it off.
- Stains caused by suntan lotion or other substances may require a commercial spot-removing product. Follow directions, then rinse well and air-dry.

Cushy Job

To help prevent moisture damage to an outdoor cushion, remove the cover if possible, protect the stuffing with a piece of plastic, then replace the cover.

DECK

- *Mold, mildew:* If you're not sure that the black spots you see are mildew, use a cotton swab to apply bleach to one of them. If the black spot disappears, it's definitely mildew. Sweep clean, then try one of the following. (They also remove berry and leaf stains.)

    Clorox Outdoor Bleach Concentrate—3 quarts make 16 gallons—has been very effective for me.

    Or use a detergent cleaner *without* ammonia, rinse with 1 part bleach to 4 parts water, then rinse with water.

    Or pour 1 cup of TSP (trisodium phosphate) and 1 cup bleach in a gallon of water, scrub mixture on deck with a hard brush, rinse after 15 minutes.
- *Fading (as a result of bleach applications or general wear) and other stains:* Use an oxalic acid–based deck restorer. (Very strong; read cautions on bottle.)
- *Grease:* Scrub with a degreasing detergent. If the stain is set in, you may need to sand with a very fine paper. Eventually the area will weather to match the surrounding deck.
- *Rust:* Use a commercial cleaner with phosphoric acid.

Phone Shed

Install a country-style mailbox on the deck or in the garden area to hold the cordless phone. You won't spill things on it, it won't get knocked to the ground, and if you forget it outside in the rain, it's covered.

Fallout Effect

- If you're using TSP, bleach, or another strong chemical, cover nearby plants so they won't be in the line of the spray or the runoff.
- A cleaner that benefits plants is lemon dishwashing soap, because it kills insects. So in the spring add 1 tablespoon to a gallon of water in a spray bottle that attaches to the hose, and spray down the garden.

PATIO DOOR SCREEN

- Get it off the track and lay it down on a soft towel. Clean it with bathroom foam cleaner without bleach. Wipe with a clean, wet cloth.
- Or leave it in place and use a paint spreader (a layer of aluminum, a layer of foam, and a layer of fuzzy material; buy one in paintbrush and roller departments). Dip the spreader in the lemon ammonia and water mixture and spread over screen. The squares of the screen will hold water to soak the other side. Wipe dry with old towels to absorb the water and the screen is clean. No drips, no hosing, no reinstalling.

MY READERS TIP ME OFF

To clean the runners in an aluminum patio door or window track, pour about ⅓ cup of diet cola in the track, spread it the full length of the track, then wipe with a rag or paper towels. Don't use regular cola, as the sugar will attract insects. The secret: the phosphoric acid in the soda.

PATIO DOOR TRACKS

- Spritz a little WD-40 in the tracks, clean with a small foam paintbrush. The tracks will be clean and the doors will move more easily too.

Patch Work

If you have holes in the screen door, make a crisis into an opportunity. Patch them with self-adhesive bathtub appliqués placed back to back. They'll hold, they're waterproof, and they'll keep people from trying to walk through the screen.

PLASTIC RESIN OUTDOOR FURNITURE

- *Grimy:* Spray with ¼ cup bleach and 1 quart of water in a spray bottle, leave, then wipe dry.

  ✪ Or, when a rainstorm is coming, spray plastic resin outdoor furniture with Fantastik. Leave it outside and let the rain do the rest.

  ✪ Or tie nylon cord around each article, then lower it into the swimming pool for 8 hours. The chlorine in your pool will clean all mildew stains and remove all dirt. (Do not try this with vinyl furniture.)

  ✪ Some stains will fade if you just leave the items in the sun.

- *Spotting:* Caused by water. Wash with mild detergent and water, rinse, then wipe dry.

MY VIEWERS TIP ME OFF

- ✪ For a quick cleanup, one woman brings all her outdoor furniture—even the umbrella—through the car wash in the back of the pickup truck.

RATTAN.

See Wicker and Rattan.

REDWOOD

- *Graying:* Some people like this effect, but if you prefer the redwood color, use semitransparent pigmented stain to restore and seal it. Prior to applying the paint, clean off surface dirt, scrub with an all-purpose cleaner, rinse, and dry. One coat is usually sufficient. Color in pigmented stains may wear away gradually after weathering. Refinishing may be necessary every 3–5 years. Use a bristle brush lightly to remove old finish in some spots.
- *Grease and soot:* Scrub with 1 cup TSP in 1 gallon of water or use Clorox Outdoor Bleach Concentrate as directed. Rinse.

STONE FLOORS (BRICK, FLAGSTONE, TERRAZZO)

- Damp-mop frequently to protect them from abrasion, and use a mild, neutral detergent. Rinse thoroughly and dry. Do not use alkaline cleaners or acids, and don't use abrasives on polished stone. Waxing any nonsmooth stone floor isn't a good idea, because it will accumulate in the niches and turn yellow; and since waxing will subsequently require stripping, it's just a lot of extra work.

Enough
^

TEAK

- Clean periodically with 4 parts liquid dish detergent or all-purpose cleaner without ammonia and 1 part bleach and a soft brush. Rinse all the solution off afterward.
- If you don't like the silver-gray, natural weathered look, buy teak cleaner from a boating or marine store.
- Teak sealer doesn't prolong the life of the wood; it's only a cosmetic treatment.

WICKER AND RATTAN

- *Grimy:* Wicker should be dusted regularly with a soft brush or vacuum brush attachment. Dirty wicker, even if it's painted, can be cleaned with warm, soapy water. Put a towel under it, or take it outside, and spray the solution using a pump sprayer from the garden supply store. Then give it a quick squirt with the hose to rinse. Don't wet to excess and don't disturb the weave pattern when it is wet by creating a gap, for example, because it will keep that pattern when it dries. Wipe dry and air-dry thoroughly for at least 24 hours before using.
- *Dry:* If it seems very dry, wipe it with a slightly damp cloth. Excessive dryness can cause splitting or warping.
- *Mildew:* Spots can be removed with a cloth dipped in diluted ammonia. The wicker won't become discolored as long as you do not saturate the wood.
- *Sagging seat:* Tighten it by washing it outdoors with hot, sudsy water. Rinse briefly with a hose and let it dry in the sun. (Don't you wish you could tighten up your *own* seat so easily?)

WROUGHT IRON

- Needs only dusting, but if you see visible grime, wash with all-purpose cleaner and hot water, rinse and dry.

When it's completely dry, you can rub it with some paste wax to make it rust-resistant, or use special paint made for this purpose.

- Remove any rust with a little white vinegar and water or a commercial rust remover.

THIRTEEN

The Quickest Cleanup Ever: Unexpected Guests Due in 30 Minutes

> **Good enough housekeeping** is knowing that tidy often goes a long way toward clean.

1. Check your outfit, comb your hair, wash your face, or fix your makeup. The first thing your guests notice isn't your living room—it's you.
2. Close doors to block off the view of whatever rooms will not be in use.
3. Carry some shopping bags into the foyer and the room you'll be using and clear the table and floor surfaces of as much clutter as possible. Hide the bag(s) somewhere out of the way—but definitely not in the coat closet, which you will probably have to open for your guests.

4. Take a light-duty spray cleaner and a few paper towels into the room you'll be using. Wipe fingerprints and other visible dirt off surfaces such as the mirror, glass-topped end table, or wooden coffee table.

5. Straighten out and fluff up the pillows on the living room furniture.

6. In the bathroom, clean up hair on the floor, toothpaste in the sink, and gunk on the mirror. Give the toilet a quick brush to avoid the Toilet of Shame. Gather up any clutter, like dirty towels, extra bottles, magazines, and so forth, and stuff it in the hamper—or just stow it behind the shower curtain. Make sure there's a clean guest towel, soap, and toilet tissue ready for your visitor(s).

7. Go into the kitchen and stow unwashed dishes in the dishwasher or oven. Clear the clutter off the counter, too. If there's no place else, stick it in the oven or the refrigerator. You may have a few minutes to finish up in here when you go into the kitchen to fix your guests a drink, but there is always the chance that a guest will follow you.

8. If you have enough time, go back and vacuum the room you'll use.

9. Spray pine cleaner all around. Dab a little behind your ears. The scent will give the impression that everything has been thoroughly scrubbed.

10. Keep this list posted where you can find it.

And that's all you need to do for now.
It's good enough!

Index

About the Authors

MARY ELLEN PINKHAM established herself as a source of useful and reliable household advice when her first book, *The Best of Helpful Hints*, shot to #1 on the *New York Times* bestseller list in 1979 and stayed there for eighteen months. After two popular follow-up books and a bestselling diet book, she became a longtime columnist for *Family Circle*, *Woman's Day*, and *Star* magazine, known for her humorous and practical approach. Mary Ellen produces and markets her own line of cleaning products and stars in *TIPical Mary Ellen* on the Home & Garden TV Network. She lives in Edina, Minnesota.

DALE BURG began her longtime collaboration with Mary Ellen Pinkham with *Mary Ellen's Help Yourself Diet Plan*, a *New York Times* bestseller in 1982. She has written sixteen books and many articles both as a collaborator and under her own name, and she had her own columns in *Family Circle* and *New Woman*, among other magazines. She has written for television and taught comedy writing. She lives in New York City.